Best Hikes Colorado's
Indian Peaks Wilderness

Best Hikes Colorado's Indian Peaks Wilderness

A Guide to the Area's Greatest
Hiking Adventures

Kent Dannen

FALCONGUIDES

GUILFORD, CONNECTICUT

In memory of Randy Bartley: brother-in-law and mountaineer.

And Jacob lifted up his feet, and he went to the land of the Bene Qedem.
Genesis 29:1

FALCONGUIDES®

An imprint of Globe Pequot
Falcon, FalconGuides, and Make Adventure Your Story are registered trademarks of Rowman & Littlefield.

Distributed by NATIONAL BOOK NETWORK

Copyright © 2017 Rowman & Littlefield
Maps by Melissa Baker © Rowman & Littlefield

British Library Cataloguing-in-Publication Information available

Library of Congress Cataloging-in-Publication Data available

Names: Dannen, Kent, 1946- author.
Title: Best hikes Colorado's Indian Peaks Wilderness : a guide to the area's greatest hiking adventures / Kent Dannen.
Description: Guilford, Connecticut : FalconGuides, [2017] | "Distributed by NATIONAL BOOK NETWORK"— T.p. verso. | Includes index.
Identifiers: LCCN 2016049550 (print) | LCCN 2017011499 (ebook) | ISBN 9781493027040 (paperback) | ISBN 9781493027057 (e-book)
Subjects: LCSH: Hiking—Colorado—Indian Peaks Wilderness—Guidebooks. | Mountaineering—Colorado—Indian Peaks Wilderness—Guidebooks. | Backpacking—Colorado—Indian Peaks Wilderness—Guidebooks. | Trails—Colorado—Indian Peaks Wilderness—Guidebooks. | Lakes—Colorado—Indian Peaks Wilderness—Guidebooks. | Colorado—Guidebooks. | Indian Peaks Wilderness (Colo.)—Guidebooks.
Classification: LCC GV199.42.C62 I53 2017 (print) | LCC GV199.42.C62 (ebook) | DDC 796.5109788—dc23
LC record available at https://lccn.loc.gov/2016049550

Printed in the United States of America

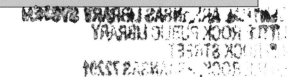

Contents

Map Overview

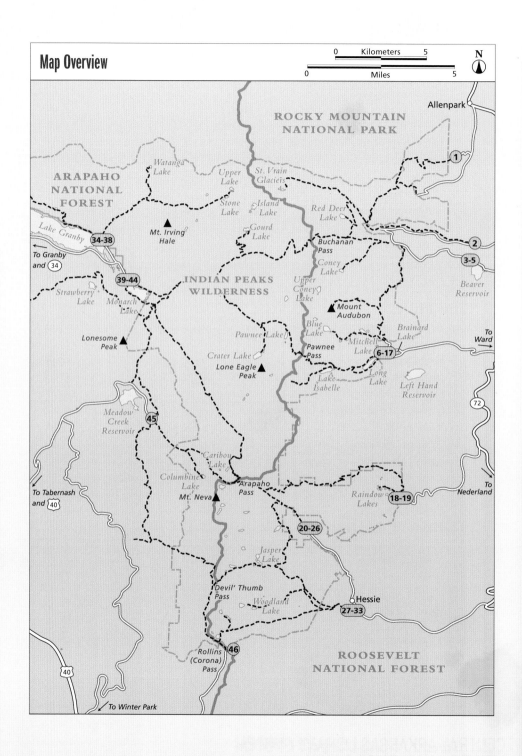

Introduction

The trails and hiking goals of Indian Peaks Wilderness are understandably popular, absolutely the equal of the hiking destinations in Rocky Mountain National Park adjacent to the north. Only the hikers are different. Colorado residents seem more common in Indian Peaks in contrast to the pedestrians drawn from all over the nation to the national park. Many of these Colorado residents are, however, rather new arrivals and as much in need of guidance as park hikers. All need to know not only how to reach wilderness goals, but also how best to share and protect the wilds. Moreover, the USDA Forest Service, which manages Indian Peaks Wilderness, has a much smaller staff with which to achieve goals very similar to those of the National Park Service within the US Department of the Interior.

The effort to create the national park was led more than a century ago by innkeeper Enos Mills, who proposed that what now is Indian Peaks be included in the national park. Indian Peaks was excluded because of the belief that not all of their significant mineral wealth had been mined. But the silver, gold, and other valuable minerals now all have been extracted, presumably.

Subsequent efforts took place in later decades to add Indian Peaks to the national park. I participated in such efforts. Local hearings indicated that I was mistaken in the attempt to shift bureaucratic responsibilities. Many comments were made that the national park attracted too many tourists who were objectionable to some locals, evidently more appreciative and deserving of unsurpassed mountain glory than were folks not so fortunate as to live in Colorado. Unaware of my innate superiority by virtue of living in Colorado, I was shocked and very unimpressed by such objections.

Much more common and reasonable was the desire to share trail experiences in Indian Peaks with leashed canine companions. Dogs, even leashed, are prohibited on trails in Rocky Mountain National Park, although not in all national parks. Despite relatively few staff members on the trail, the Forest Service has managed to achieve acceptably high compliance with a necessary (for the best experience of both human and canine hikers) leash regulation, as use of Indian Peaks trails boomed when the area achieved wilderness protection. (Note further comments about dogs on trails in the Pets section below.)

Another difference between Indian Peaks Wilderness and Rocky Mountain National Park is that wildlife seems more abundant in the park. This is likely due to hunting prohibition within the park as well as on surrounding land. Hunting is permitted in Indian Peaks, although removing slain prey can be difficult because motorized vehicles are not permitted, thereby increasing the labor of removing game. Spectacular wildflower display is significantly more obvious in Indian Peaks than in the national park. It may be that this contrast between plant and animal populations in the two adjacent areas is not coincidental.

Wildflowers are particularly abundant along the trail to Woodland Lake.

In contrast to Rocky Mountain National Park, no roads (such as Trial Ridge or Old Fall River roads) traverse the passes among the Indian Peaks. This lack of very easy access, except at Rollins Pass (also called Corona Pass), to the alpine tundra in Indian Peaks is offset somewhat by some trailheads beginning at relatively high altitudes. Railroad and wagon road routes of the past have disintegrated to pleasant trails.

How to Use This Guide: With Great Diligence

Indian Peaks is one of the most heavily visited areas preserved under the protection of the Wilderness Act of 1964. This enlightened legislation recognizes the value of land that remains essentially in its wild state, unaltered by humankind. Such values are spiritual, recreational, and economic in nature.

Indian Peaks Wilderness is particularly noteworthy because it succeeds in preserving these values despite its numerous visitors (far exceeding 100,000 hikers per year) and relatively few USDA Forest Service personnel to manage it. Since my first experience on Indian Peaks trails, the natural, wild environment in a time of greatly increased use has become less battered by humankind, wilder, more beautiful, and more valuable for uplifting the human spirit.

Even I find such good news difficult to believe as I write it. But I have seen it happen. This near miracle has come about because the average Indian Peaks visitor is more sophisticated and concerned about wilderness values than is normal among humans.

I write "average" and "normal." Angelic behavior is not universal. Few Indian Peaks hikers have their heads circled by halos or walk with the wisdom of long experience. But many are everyday folk who have been lucky enough to have been made aware of the nature of wilderness and their ethical responsibility to not harm it. Many of these fortunately enlightened people volunteer their precious time (when they otherwise could be pushing their own way further into the wilderness) to train with and cooperate with the Forest Service in leading fellow visitors along paths of righteous wilderness care.

The forty-six hikes described in this guide are mostly along trails until, in some cases, a final rock scramble to a summit. Some of the most popular of these trails wind through forests that are mature and extraordinarily lovely because they receive so much water from melting snow. Some of this meltwater ends up on trails, making them sloppy, sometimes well into July.

In the J. R. R. Tolkien epic, hobbits hiking through Mirkwood are told to "Stay on the trail!" They do not follow these instructions, and problems ensue. The thousands of Indian Peaks hikers likely will not face goblins or giant spiders if they leave the trail, but they will face degradation of spectacular wilderness forest by pounding parallel trails into ground cover that is essential to wilderness charm and wildlife food. So, stay on the trail even if you have to tramp through mud.

Each hike description begins with decision-making data to help you determine whether this hike is for you. Following a short overview, you will find where the hike begins, predicted hiking time (a semi-wild guess), distance, difficulty, trail surface (mostly dirt with some rocks on which to trip), elevation, best season to make the hike, other trail users, whether you can bring your pet (yes, if it is a leashed dog; the leash is a very big deal if we are to continue to enjoy canine companionship and help), whether a fee or permit is required, trail contacts for additional information, useful topographic maps (in addition to the maps provided in this book), trail highlights, and wildlife you might encounter.

Indian Peaks extend north below airplane toward Rocky Mountain National Park.

None of the hikes are necessarily better than the others on any particular day, but they do differ in difficulty and accessibility. Unsurprisingly, long hikes are harder than short hikes. If distances are similar, hikes that go to mountain summits are harder than those that do not. Some hikes are redundant with other (longer) hikes. For instance, you go to Mitchell Lake on the way to Blue Lake.

Following the at-a-glance information, you will find directions to the trailhead.

The Hike describes why you would want to spend precious time on an even more precious experience. Following each hike description, the Miles and Directions section provides a mile-by-mile summary of junctions and major landmarks along the trail. Sidebars throughout the guide highlight some aspects of Indian Peaks Wilderness that help make it so wonderful.

Transportation

Access to Indian Peaks trailheads is limited to private vehicles. In some cases, high clearance and four-wheel drive (4WD) vehicles are more secure if not absolutely necessary. Fuel is not available near some trailheads; a full tank will provide ease of mind.

Indian Peaks Commemorate Indian History

For 25 years, when botany teacher Ellsworth Bethel looked out of his classroom window at East Denver High School, he admired the ragged line of mountains between

Longs Peak south to Arapaho Peaks. During his last year of teaching in 1914, he decided that South and North Arapaho peaks were well-named and that the peaks to the north likewise should be named for Indian tribes. With some dispute about details, his idea met with broad agreement.

On May 14, 1914, Bethel sent his suggestions for appropriate names to the US Board on Geographic Names in Washington, D. C. Most of the tribal names approved by the board had some connection with Colorado history. The system seemed so appropriate that many hikers and climbers, in what came to be known as Indian Peaks Wilderness, began to apply names of additional tribes unofficially to other rocky prominences in the vicinity.

More than a dozen tribes resided in Colorado, with some represented on Indian Peaks and others not. All the ancestral Puebloan tribes tend to be lumped together in this dozen, which is at least linguistically inaccurate. Current knowledge does not permit finer distinction among the Pueblos who once lived in literally countless places in southwest Colorado, as far north as Chimney Rocks. The Pueblos left the state before Europeans arrived.

In alphabetical (rather than Indian Peaks hiking) order, Colorado tribes are as follows.

Apache bands raided or wandered occasionally into Colorado. Only the Jicarilla Apache lived permanently within present state boundaries. Jicarilla is a name given by Mexican Spaniards because Jicarilla women made particularly fine baskets. All Apache tribes spoke a language of the Athapascan linguistic stock, indicating that they originated in southwestern Canada, likely moving south along the eastern base of the Rockies. The Jicarilla version of the Apache language differed somewhat from other Apache groups except Lipan in Texas. Apache Peak is prominent along the Continental Divide in the very familiar view above Lake Isabelle.

The Spanish explorer Coronado likely met Apaches in 1540 to 1542. He called them (as well as other tribes) Querechos. Later, Spanish explorers used the name Vaqueros. The Apache relations with European descendants and other Indian tribes were classically hostile, although less so in Colorado.

The **Arapaho** tribe took up the now classic horse-nomad lifestyle after the Spanish introduced horses to the Great Plains from the south and the French introduced guns from the north. Prior to this conversion, the Arapaho likely lived a sedentary life in the Red River Valley in Minnesota. At a time and place unclear, they allied themselves with Cheyenne horse-nomads. Like the Cheyenne, the Arapaho divided into northern and southern groups, the southern groups drawn down to the Arkansas River to take advantage of trade in bison hides, centered at Bent's Fort after 1832 (today near La Junta, Colorado). Although horse-nomad tribes typically relied on bison hunting for their basic food, both the allies and enemies of the Arapaho often called them "dog eaters," which would make them unpopular among a large percentage of modern hikers who benefit from canine companionship in Indian Peaks.

Although not a Colorado tribe, the **Arikara** were used as a map label in Indian Peaks (spelled Arikaree). These farmers along the Missouri River were an offshoot of the Pawnee. Arikara may have been responsible for carrying knowledge of growing corn to other agricultural tribes along the Missouri, including the Mandan and Hidatsa. These three tribes eventually united after all were drastically depopulated by European disease and by war with nomads on European-introduced horses.

The **Bannock** tribe joined with the Shoshoni in wandering over the northwestern corner of Colorado from their main homeland in Idaho and Wyoming. The Bannock are not represented on Indian Peaks geographic features.

The **Cheyenne,** before 1700, lived in Minnesota as farmers of corn and other edible plants. With the advent of Europeans with horses and guns, the Cheyenne took up a nomadic lifestyle based on hunting bison. After the Bent brothers built a fur-trading fort along the Arkansas River in Colorado in 1832, the Cheyenne divided into distinct northern and southern tribes. When away from the Bents' pacifying influence (no trade goods to fighters), the southern Cheyenne fought with the Kiowa until 1840, when they decided to ally with these other horse-nomads to fight Euro-Americans and other tribes. Significantly, the names used by enemy tribes for the Cheyenne were based on distinctive decoration painted on their arrows.

The name Cheyenne comes from a Dakota (Sioux) word meaning "red talkers," meaning that the northern Cheyenne spoke a different language from the Dakota with whom they joined to fight Euro-Americans. Major Colorado conflicts between Euro-Americans and Cheyenne included the infamous Sand Creek Massacre of a peaceful Cheyenne village and subsequent fights with decidedly unpeaceful Cheyenne at Beecher Island near today's Wray and Summit Springs near Sterling.

The Cheyenne tribe is not present on an Indian Peaks map because the tribe's name is used on other features in Colorado. However, an individual Cheyenne named Hiamovi has provided a name for a mountain and lake in the wilderness, standing in for the rest of his people.

The **Dakota,** unsurprisingly, lived in the present states of North and South Dakota as well as Montana, Wyoming, Nebraska, and Minnesota. French fur traders called them Sioux, based on a Chippewa word for enemy. The bulk of this large tribe became among the most famous of horse-nomads when European introduction of horses and guns made the hard life of farming seem much less appealing. Some Dakota ventured south to wage war in support of their Cheyenne allies. There were Dakota warriors at the famous Beecher Island fight between US Army scouts and Cheyenne near today's Wray, Colorado.

Neither Dakota nor Sioux appear in Indian Peaks. But on the northern edge of the wilderness at the border with Rocky Mountain National Park is Ogalalla Peak, named for a famous division of the tribe (sometimes spelled Oglala) that included the war leader Crazy Horse.

Evidently always a plains tribe, the **Comanche** readily switched to horse-nomad culture, as did former farmers like the Dakota, Arapaho, and Cheyenne. The Comanche were particularly famous for their relatively large population, equestrian skills, and inclination toward war. They resided north of the Arkansas River before moving south to fight Spaniards, Apaches, and particularly Texans. They also were major horse traders, speeding the spread of horses from their source in Mexico to tribes on the northern plains. The Comanche tribe provides no label in Indian Peaks, but a Comanche Peak rises along the northern boundary of Rocky Mountain National Park.

The **Kiowa**'s early home was the headwaters of the Missouri River in Montana. Intertribal warfare forced them south to the Arkansas River in Colorado. After making peace with the Comanche south of the river, the Kiowa continued south, and thereafter allied with the Comanche against Mexicans and Texans. Their wide-ranging nomadic life took them into Colorado's eastern plains. Usually roaming with the Kiowa was the **Kiowa Apache** band of the Kiowa, which spoke a dialect related to Apache, but who were otherwise unconnected to the Apache. Kiowa Peak rises in Indian Peaks along the Continental Divide, and Satanta Peak (named for a famous Kiowa war leader) stands to the west across the valley of Arapaho Creek.

The **Navajo** tribe is closely associated with Colorado's southern boundary. Their culture also was radically altered by European arrival, but as herders of sheep and goats rather than as horse-nomads. The US Army enlisted a prominent Colorado mountain man, Kit Carson, to end Navajo raids on Pueblos and Euro-Americans. This he accomplished by killing most of the Navajo sheep and goats and confining the tribe where the army could keep an eye on them. In 1867, the Navajo were restored to their homeland and given new sheep and goats. Subsequently, they multiplied to one of the largest of Native American tribes, famous for their blankets made from wool yarn as well as for distinctive jewelry. Also distinctive is the conical shape of Navajo Peak, perhaps the most familiar reference point along the Continental Divide in Indian Peaks.

The **Pawnee** were a mostly sedentary tribe living in various agricultural villages of dome-shaped earth lodges, particularly in Nebraska and Kansas. They did prey on bison while the corn was maturing, and they hunted on Colorado's eastern plains between the South Platte and Arkansas rivers. Because Pawnee villages were designed to be permanent, the horse-nomads always knew where to go to steal corn, the taste for which they had not entirely abandoned when adopting their roaming lifestyle. Warfare between Indian farmers and horse-nomads was constant, and the Pawnee allied themselves with the US Army. The Pawnee are represented in Indian Peaks Wilderness on a summit along the Continental Divide as well as a pass and lake below that summit.

Pueblo people heavily occupied southwestern Colorado prior to their departure to New Mexico before Europeans arrived. Remains of ancestral Puebloan buildings are a major attraction for travelers to Colorado. These structures and their builders are explained at Mesa Verde National Park, Hovenweep and Chimney Rock national monuments, Lowry Pueblo in Canyon of the Ancients National Monument, and the Anasazi Heritage Center.

The **Shoshoni**, in company with the Bannock, wandered over the far northwestern corner of Colorado. Another branch of the tribe allied itself with Euro-Americans against traditional enemies such as Dakota, Cheyenne, and Arapaho. The Shoshoni managed to give up fighting with the Crow when they united against other horse-nomads. Shoshoni Peak is on a sharp eastern spur of the Continental Divide, making it particularly prominent from the very popular trail to Long Lake and Lake Isabelle.

The **Ute** tribe occupied most of central and western Colorado and became embroiled in one major war with Euro-Americans. There is no Ute Peak in Indian Peaks because the name already had been applied to geographical features elsewhere. The name Paiute was substituted even though Paiutes originally were more speakers of a common dialect than a tribe and did not live in Colorado.

Although not entirely pleased with the way his naming scheme for Indian Peaks came to pass, Ellsworth Bethel hopefully came to be mostly satisfied by the time he died in 1925. Indian Peaks Wilderness welcomes more hikers on its trails than most other wilderness areas in the United States. Doubtless, most of those thousands of pedestrians think Bethel had a pretty good idea.

Before the Indians: Geology of Indian Peaks

The books that record and protect the creation stories of the people for whom Indian Peaks Wilderness is named would fill a rather long shelf. These often are called creation myths. In this case, myth is a technical term that does not mean the stories are untrue, but rather that they represent supernatural understanding beyond the realm of ordinary sensory perception. Many Navajo myths are particularly well-known and popular. In a Navajo creation myth, Begochiddy (the child of the sun) first created four mountains. Just how the mountains were created varies among Navajo stories.

As it happens, just how mountains were created varies among modern geological explanations, according to what kind of mountains are being described. As in he Navajo myths, there are different mountains in different places that came to be in different ways. Sixty-five to forty-five million years ago, plates of solid earth on the relatively thin crust above a mass of molten rock within the earth were floating on convection currents moved by the heat of the molten rock. Two of these plates, called naturally enough the North American Plate and the Pacific Plate, bumped into each other. The Pacific Plate was (and is) denser and heavier than the North American Plate. Therefore, in the crash (a relative term for movement about as fast as your fingernail grows), the Pacific Plate was pushed under the lighter North American Plate. The edge of the Pacific Plate descended into the hot earth, was liquefied, and migrated to the western side of the Pacific to be regurgitated as magma in the mid-Pacific to begin its conveyor belt journey to North America. The response of the North American Plate was to rise to the east of where the Pacific Plate plunged beneath it. Thus, the mountains along the west side of North America came, by uplift and volcanic eruption, to be caused by such violent geology.

Disturbance of North America also occurred further inland from the crash zone as a succession of mountains towered as far east as today's Indian Peaks. Various geologists suggest at least four explanations of why the Colorado Rockies rose to more than 14,000 feet higher than where the Pacific Plate dove under North America. Paralleling Begochiddy's initial creation of four mountains, geologists prove themselves to be as imaginative story tellers as the Navajo.

Although geologic explanations of Rocky Mountains uplift differ, consensus dominates the story of how the Rockies and other mountains are torn down. The sun (geologists do not claim solar parentage of Begochiddy) evaporates water into the air. Water droplets condense on very tiny particles of dust in the air and precipitate as rain or snow, bit by bit eroding the mountain, sometimes for so long as to make the rough places a plain. Navajo Peak, according to the geological creation story, eroded from its most recent high point to an elevation of 13,409 feet. This seems very high but is less high than Navajo was 65 million years ago.

Tribal explanations of Begochiddy creating the mountains or of Coyote (a clever deity) singing the peaks into place are safer than geologic explanation, which is a dizzying tale. Dizziness is dangerous when climbing or hiking in Indian Peaks.

Geology also tells us that Navajo Peak received its current cone shape from being carved and plucked by glaciers, the last major episode being approximately between 1400 and 1850, during what is called the Little Ice Age. These glaciers formed during cold ages when the sun spread less heat on the earth than at other times due to the earth's somewhat erratic orbit. Some speculation adds that decrease in human population (in the Eastern Hemisphere) due to disease may have permitted regrowth of forests, thereby consuming more carbon dioxide during the Little Ice Age and reducing the amount of greenhouse warming effect of CO_2 trapping heat from the sun within the earth's atmosphere.

Because wind generally blows from the west, it carried snow to dump where the wind no longer could reach it on the east side of the mountains. Thus, glaciers tended to form on the east-facing sides of the peaks, causing more dramatic carving on the east than on the west. Navajo Peak, however, happened to be located relative to other mountains in such a way that it was carved rather similarly on all sides, making it easy for hikers to identify Navajo, no matter from what direction they happen to view it within Indian Peaks.

When the depth of accumulated snow (which evolved to ice) reached at least 250 feet, the weight of the ice caused it to flow downhill through valleys previously carved by flowing water. The slowly moving sheets of ice would freeze to rock walls and pull off large and small pieces as it moved. More carving was accomplished as the pieces of rock that were plucked or just fell onto the ice from surrounding cliffs acted as rasps on a file within the moving ice. This plucking and filing occurred not only on the valley walls ever steepened by the passing glacier, but also on the valley floor, gouging out basins. The steep walls and broad floors give glacier-carved valleys an obvious U profile.

Depending on how far down to lower (warmer) altitude the glacier flowed and on how long the cold age lasted, these mountain glaciers eventually stopped flowing. At that point, a melting conveyor belt of ice dumped the rock it was carrying at its end. This dumped rock piled up in a ridge called a terminal moraine. Rock carried along the edges of the glacier was dumped to form lateral moraines when the glacier melted (retreated) back up the valley. The back-and-forth movement of ice was not steady. Sometimes, a glacier would retreat up a valley to a certain point and stop for centuries. At this new end of the glacier, a rock ridge would accumulate to form a recessional moraine. When the ice melted, the moraines often formed dams behind which melted ice or subsequent precipitation accumulated, creating lakes. Lakes also formed in the basins plucked from the valley floor by moving ice.

A line of such lakes formed along the valley floors and connected by a stream flowing from one lake to another is called a "paternoster lake." Observed from surrounding peaks and passes, the lakes (formed in identical fashion in European mountains) were thought to resemble paternoster beads strung together as a memory aid when reciting prayers. *Pater noster* is Latin for our father, the opening words of the Lord's Prayer.

Recessional and terminal moraines are small ridges marked by lines of shrubby plants and unnamed pond below Caribou Pass. Much-eroded lateral moraine on right indicates furthest advance of glacier, likely during the Little Ice Age between 1400 and 1850.

Indian Peaks Wilderness still contains mountain glaciers, but they have melted almost away during the current warm period and are doing very little carving now. Arapaho Glacier, on the east flanks of South and North Arapaho peaks is the farthest south glacier in the Rocky Mountains. That it still exists has been considered a geological wonder.

To me the most interesting example of glacial moraines is one of the youngest, likely formed during the Little Ice Age, tiny, and perched very obviously below Caribou Pass. A terminal moraine hangs on the valley wall at the head of Arapaho Creek. Just yards inside the arc of the terminal moraine, is a recessional moraine, taller than its eroded predecessor, mimicking its arc, and enclosing a glacial lake. A lateral moraine indicates the farthest extent of this glacier's advance.

Historically, the most significant aspect of Indian Peaks' geology has been the very rich deposits of valuable minerals, the mining of which began in 1859. For more than half a century, silver west of Nederland and gold around Ward outshone the area's dramatic scenery. The Indian Peaks mineral deposits are at the north end of the Colorado mineral belt, a band of historically valuable mines about 50 miles wide stretching to the southwest part of the state. It seems that Indian Peaks and most of the rest of the mineral belt have given up all of their valuable minerals, leaving the aboveground, visual wealth mostly pristine.

Weather. It's Usually Good for Hiking

Weather in Indian Peaks Wilderness is no easier to predict than weather anywhere else. Nonetheless, some guesses can be useful for hikers.

During the summer, afternoon rain is common. Storms usually come from the west. Storms that arrive from the east tend to be particularly nasty. An early start to any destination is a good idea. East of the peaks, early means enough before sunrise to catch the prettiest light at your destination. Approaches from the west tend to be lengthier; it might be worthwhile to try to time your arrival at the best scenery for the theoretical time after rain has passed.

Of course, you do not want to be above tree line in a storm. Plan to reach summits and be off before noon. Assume that storms from any direction are malevolent. Lightning tries the hardest to kill you. But wind, wet, and cold are waiting to attack should lightning miss. Mountain pine beetles have killed countless lodgepole pines on the west side of Indian Peaks, and wind can blow them onto the unwary or unlucky.

Despite the danger of falling trees during a storm, there is more safety below tree line than above. Besides lightning danger, falling snow can assault you at high altitude any day of the year. Precipitation might be only an inconvenience if you carry warm and water repellent clothing. But, wet rocks are slick and perversely seem even more so at cliff edges.

Some hikers decide to ignore bad weather. For many others, the discomfort of storms causes their minds to work less well. Failing to recognize, respect, and retreat from bad weather is foolish and maybe fatal.

On the other hand, a cloudless, bright sunshiny day may ultimately pose greater risk than storm clouds. Lightning might miss you; ultraviolet radiation will not. Do not decide whether or not to apply sunscreen well before the UV hits you. Just smear it on as a matter of policy, no matter what your judgment about the weather. And wear a hat that shades your face. Colorado's abundant sunshine and thin air give this state the nation's highest rate of skin cancer. It might result from cumulative exposure, but it might also result from a one-time burn.

Many of these weather precautions apply to outdoor activity everywhere. Indian Peaks weather normally is shockingly pleasant.

Flora

Horizontal bands of different plant communities wrap all high mountains at different elevations. Indian Peaks Wilderness contains three such bands of life, called by botanists the montane zone, the subalpine zone, and the alpine zone.

The montane zone is most evident on the lower western trails of Indian Peaks, dominated by lodgepole pines. Lumber operations a century ago around Monarch Lake may have removed ponderosa pines, a major lumber tree, and signature tree of montane forests. The present lodgepole pines (beset by a beetle-carried fungus, likely abundant due to global warming of the industrial age) would be a typical species to follow removed ponderosas, or lodgepole might have predominated in the first place. In either case, stiff winds from the west have many opportunities to blow dead lodgepole pines across trails. Be grateful if you have to climb over them rather than attempt to dodge them as they fall.

Approximately 10,000 feet above sea level, the subalpine zone takes over with big trees, notably subalpine fir and Engelmann spruce. Both are short-needled conifers with needles that grow singly (not in clumps) along the branches. Fir needles are soft to the touch; spruce needles are sharp. Spruce cones, on the other hand, are soft with papery scales and often cover the floor of a thick forest. Fir cones are only rarely seen on the ground, likely having been cut by a red squirrel to store for future food. Growing black and pitchy at the tops of firs, the fir cones disintegrate in place to spread their seeds widely, leaving spiky cone cores standing upright in the tops of the trees.

In the heart of the subalpine zone, the spruce and fir grow close together, tall and massive. They are watered by melting snowbanks that are deepest in the subalpine forest because winter wind drops snow snatched from the summits to lower altitude, where the snow is protected from wind and sun.

However, the trees get shorter as the altitude gets higher. At tree line, near 11,500 feet, wind sculpts the trees into its own self-portrait, called krummholz ("elfen wood"), by killing whatever branches and twigs are most exposed to winter gales.

Lodgepole pine also extends into the subalpine zone, particularly where fires have cleared away other species. With thin bark, lodgepoles are subject to being killed by fire. But, death of mature lodgepoles removes shade, opening the forest floor to sunshine beloved by baby lodgepoles. Furthermore, the extreme heat of wildfire causes tightly closed lodgepole cones to open, shedding long-stored seeds over a freshly prepared bed.

Lodgepole trunks tend to be tall, uniform, and skinny. They often grow crowded together in aptly named "doghair" stands and can make rather monotonous surroundings for trails. However, these forests provided very useful trunks that formed the structures of tipis; hence, they are called lodgepoles.

More individually interesting in subalpine forests are limber pines. Their clumps of five needles give character to flexible limber pine branches. Their flexibility allows wind to twist limber pines into the most dramatic of tree line forms.

Where long ago winds, fires, or avalanches have opened meadows in the forests, ages of organic soil accumulation support wildly colorful displays of subalpine flowers, masses of yellow composites, magenta primroses, red and yellow Indian paintbrush, and blue chiming bells. Their relatively large blossoms are watered by melting snow protected in nearby forest shade. Normally, these are the most dramatic and memorable flower displays in the mountains.

However, the tiny ground-hugging flowers above tree line (alpine zone) also have their champions among hikers who climb above 11,500 feet. These jewel-like blossoms are rugged heroes, celebrating life at its harshest. The winds that scour this alpine tundra environment at more than 100 mph are determined that nothing living shall control the heights. But from the banner trees at tree line, life crawls forward, finding bits of shelter from the wind. Commonly such shelters are rocks, but some plants build their own wind havens. They grow in roughly spherical shapes to shed the wind and grab bits of soil the wind carries. As soil accumulates beneath these "cushion plants," it provides a place for less-pioneer-like flowers to take root and sometimes spread a carpet of life across the rocky mountain summits.

Spotted frequently across these tundra carpets are rocks, which should be used as stepping stones when possible. The tundra plants, although very tough, are often called delicate because their environment is so harsh that it takes little additional stress to kill them. Therefore, if a trail exists across a tundra landscape, use it, confining the damage to where it already exists. Hike in single file. Where no trail exists, spread out, using rocks when available to disperse the wear and tear.

Fauna

I have heard of a mountain lion following hikers down the path from Blue Lake, one of Indian Peaks' most popular trails. When the hikers reached the parking lot, the lion went off to do other lion things, leaving the hikers with a "wouldn't-trade-anything-for-it" memory.

Aside from my wishing that I had been part of that hiking group, this is a rather dull story, dull because nothing much happened. Nothing much happened because the hikers stuck together, and no child was running alone to attract a hungry or pregnant lion. Nothing much happened because Indian Peaks trails often host hikers accompanied by leashed dogs, reducing the target value of all human hikers whether

Mountain lion cubs tussle in play.

or not they are connected to a canine companion. Nothing much happened because the "Peaceable Kingdom" theme of many American paintings inspired by prophetic words in the Bible's *Isaiah* 11:6-9 really is possible. The theme of the paintings is that the two-legged and four-legged creatures can live together in harmony.

It is true, but for hikers on Indian Peaks' trails, this happy harmony will be best preserved if a little child does not lead them, run ahead, and get eaten. Fewer than a dozen people in the United States have been killed by lions during the last century. But I remember two of them in Colorado. Both were kids running mindlessly alone in a typical kid fashion.

The terrain surrounding the trail to Blue Lake is not ideal lion habitat. But, with individual mountain lion ranges varying in size between 10 and 370 square miles, ideal may not be a particularly relevant concern. It is possible, though unlikely, to encounter lions (traveling under alternative names such as puma, cougar, or panther) anywhere in Indian Peaks. The 7- to 8-foot cat's most obvious feature may be its long tail, an answer to the question "Was that a lion or a [much smaller] bobcat?"

If you are lucky enough to spot a lion, try to pick up a sturdy stick without bending over. A bending or stooped posture might encourage attack, but getting a sturdy stick in hand while standing up may pose a problem. Many hikers carry their own staffs, which serve many purposes. But, given the extreme rarity of lions, such staffs are far more likely to prevent a broken bone in a fall than a lion attack. Snatch up

Black bears may visit campsites in Indian Peaks.

any little kids and tell them to keep quiet, for young, high voices may sound like prey. Grabbing a child and telling the child to keep still may be in the same category of difficulty as picking up a stick or stone without bending over. Do not turn your back on a lion; rather, talk calmly but forcefully and back away slowly. Of course, walking backwards makes falling over a rock or stump likely, inciting lion attack. The bigger you are, the less you look like prey; standing up straight and spreading your arms wide, holding open a jacket if you are wearing one, might be useful. Of course, it is hard to hold a child in your arms if they are spread wide to increase your size.

Although it seems there is no sure way to scare off a lion, this is not true. Hiking with a dog is very likely to discourage a lion from being anywhere close because wolves are lions' only significant natural enemies. Hiking in a group will have the same effect. However, the surest way to make a lion go away is to lift your camera to your eye with dreams of a prize-winning photo. You might capture an image of the end a very long tail disappearing into the trees.

More imposing and certainly bigger than a lion is a moose. Once wiped out in Colorado, moose have reappeared in their natural range since reintroduction in 1978. The largest of deer, these dark giants move with surprising agility and grace and are always surprising when they materialize on a trail. They are most inclined to belliger-ence in fall (during rut) and even then usually will not charge unless pressed.

Moose do constitute another reason to keep dogs leashed. A leashed dog may keep your heart in your chest by alerting you to moose presence before the startle factor takes away whatever breath the thin air permits in your lungs. Even more important, the leash will prevent a dog pushed by its wolf genes from coming too close to potentially deadly hooves.

Other "I-can't-wait-to-tell-my-friends-about-this" wildlife inhabitants of Indian Peaks are black bears. They are not only black, sometimes rolling along in dark brown or even yellowish-cinnamon. They are very much more inclined to flee than to attack. But, they can be obstinate about the rights to a log or rock they have overturned for the yummy creepy-crawlies underneath. The same principle can apply to a berry patch in the fall or a hiker's pack containing something edible.

In campgrounds on the edges of Indian Peaks, keeping anything remotely edible (even toothpaste) in a car trunk is adequate precaution. Hard-sided trailers or recreational vehicles are safe. Some campsites come equipped with bear lockers. Within the wilderness, suspend all edibles in a bag at least 10 feet above the ground and 4 feet from any tree trunk. Black bears are clever acrobats. Because it will be difficult to find a handy branch that you can throw a line over, carry two lines—one to string between trees at a level 12 feet above the ground (to offset the stretching of the line under weight) and one for suspending the food bag. Preparing and eating food well away from where you sleep is also a good precaution. A deodorizing spray may help eliminate odors of food from your camp. Also avoid wearing clothes that have food spilled on them. Of course, if bears do not equate people with easy food, you will see the bears much less often. Most hikers think this is a worthwhile tradeoff to keep the bears from being destroyed.

Because black bears tend to avoid people, are more active at night than in daytime, and have excellent sight and sense of smell, happening across them under normal, non-food-related circumstances is rare. Such encounters usually occur in the very early morning or late evening. Ideally, both hiker and bear will immediately about-face and head noisily away from each other. (This is unlikely to incite a predator response in the black bear.)

The chances of accidentally coming between a mother bear and her cubs are very low. However, if you should be relaxing against a tree when bark and needles come down on you, look up. If you see two incredibly cute cubs above you where mother has sent them for safekeeping, depart at once.

Black bears, normally solitary creatures, come together to mate in spring. The cubs are not born until the following winter, during the mother's long sleep. Normally there are two; they weigh only about 8–10 ounces and are mostly naked. Mom is too sleepy to do much for them except provide rich milk. By the time mother and cubs emerge from the winter den, the cubs are covered with hair and weigh 4–20 pounds.

Bear cubs have great fun playing with each other during the summer. However, the mother is a strict disciplinarian and tries to keep them from being eaten by larger predators, including old male black bears. The cubs soon can climb trees, nearly as well as squirrels, and spend much time in the upper branches, while their mother is feeding. Cubs often sleep high in a tree. The mother bear needs more than a year to instruct her young on how to live a safe bear life. The cubs usually split from their mother after the second summer. They may winter together, but the following spring go their separate ways.

Bear signs that hikers may encounter include scratch marks on soft-barked aspen trunks. Bears use trails for the same reasons humans do, but are not shy about leaving feces on trails, sizable droppings that often are full of hair, plant leaves, partially digested berries, or seeds. Bear tracks are distinctive and somewhat resemble human footprints.

The rear paw is about 7 inches long; the front paw is short and approximately 4–5 inches wide. Claws may or may not show up in the prints.

Coyotes play a cultural role in Indian Peaks as a frequent participant in stories that explain how things came to be. Unsurprisingly, the creative power of these "song dogs" often is expressed as occurring through singing. These tales, however, also stress coyote cleverness.

Ravens occupy a leading part in Native American stories. Like most of the corvid family (crows and jays), ravens are notably smart, which likely accounts for their prominence in creation stories. Ravens are very common in the West, where vacationers from the East often mistake them for crows. Ravens are bigger than crows, but without a nearby crow for comparison, size is not an easy identification point. Just assuming that all soaring black birds are ravens is not too unreasonable, but there are crows in these mountains too. Look at the bills and tails. Raven bills are noticeably massive, and their tails are wedge-shaped.

The most noticeable critter among Indian Peaks wildlife is the red squirrel or chickaree. The race in Indian Peaks is more brown than red. They are smaller than tree squirrels with which many hikers are familiar as rodents around their homes. Their chatter at humans they regard as trespassers in their subalpine woods is heard by all Indian Peaks hikers who are not completely oblivious to their surroundings. Chickarees are not as inherently tame as chipmunks or golden-mantled ground squirrels. But they are fearless enough to present close-up views of their bushy tails held over backs while they nibble on cones for seeds. The cone scales that accumulate below favored perches are called "squirrel kitchens," and the squirrels often bury cones for future use within these piles.

Wilderness

Wilderness is a technical term as used in the Wilderness Act of 1964. This landmark law for preservation of a precious status for wild lands defines wilderness very specifically. Congress created Indian Peaks Wilderness in 1978. The USDA Forest Service manages most of this wilderness of 17,586 acres. A subsequent boundary change to conform to natural features shifted a small part of Indian Peaks Wilderness into Rocky Mountain National Park, which administers it in a way similar in most respects to Forest Service administration. Assisting the Forest Service are the Indian Peaks Wilderness Alliance and Grand County Wilderness Group volunteers, who educate wilderness visitors along trails about destinations and appropriate wilderness use and preservation.

Wilderness Access Fees

Driving to the most popular trailheads in Indian Peaks, in the vicinity of Brainard Lake, requires a fee of $10.00. A National Parks and Federal Recreation Lands Pass (a lifetime pass for persons 62 years or older) costs $10.00 and will get pass holder and companions in a private vehicle past the fee collection station. Parking for most trailheads on the west side of Indian Peaks also requires a fee of $5.00 for daily use or a multiagency pass. These should be displayed on either the dashboard or rearview mirror.

Leashed Samoyed pack dog points out trailside elk bed to a hiker who would not have noticed it if the dog had not been attached to her.

Pets

The most noticeable difference between administration of Indian Peaks Wilderness and the national park to the north is that the Forest Service permits hiking with leashed dogs on Indian Peaks trails.

My hiking policy is to always keep my dogs protected by leashes, even outside Indian Peaks Wilderness, even on trails where leashing is not required. Too often (once is too often) I have seen a notice written on whatever paper was available and fixed in some manner to trailhead signs requesting help in finding a lost dog. Such notices inspire my anger and sorrow and convert my hike to a lost dog search. I never have succeeded.

There are hikers who maintain that their unleashed dogs are under voice control (they come when called). I find this claim in event of sudden appearance of deer, elk, or squirrel to be highly dubious. I am sorry my fellow obedience trial competitors; I just do not believe voice control is sufficiently certain for safety. I even have seen my leashed dog looking up from sniffing an Indian Peaks trail with quills from an absent porcupine piercing her nose.

Perhaps the most certain advantage of keeping dogs leashed on any trail, whether required or not, is that having them attached practically guarantees that you will expand your observation of trailside events and wonders. Keeping a dog within 6 feet makes you far more likely to share the superior canine senses of hearing and smell. Wilderness preservation saints such as John Muir, Enos Mills, and Aldo Leopold fervently proclaimed the benefits of sense sharing with dogs while hiking. Leopold was the most significant advocate for protection of wilderness areas such as Indian Peaks. His daughter told me that Aldo Leopold came to understand the importance of wilderness because he was humble enough to learn from his dogs. Modern hikers insightful enough to learn from the writings of pioneering champions for the wilds will learn of their enthusiasm for dogs on the trails. Hikers who fail to acknowledge such wisdom will do well to learn the humility of Aldo Leopold.

Another important benefit of constant adherence to the leash regulation is to protect this essential permission for hikers to enjoy the wilderness with all the benefits of canine companionship. Deciding to allow a dog to run free is a misguided attempt to boost the dog's enjoyment of the wilds, which not only endangers the dog but also endangers continued permission for leashed dogs to accompany their owners and greatly expand their appreciation of wilderness values.

Camping

Camping permits are required in Indian Peaks Wilderness in order to reduce wear on the wilderness and wear on campers from too many people attempting to camp near each other. Permits (for which a small fee is required) and rules for camping are available online and from Forest Service offices at 2140 Yarmouth Ave., Boulder 80301 (north side of town along US 36) and 9 Ten Mile Dr., PO Box 10, Granby 80446 (south side of Granby). Permits also are available at Indian Peaks Ace Hardware at Nederland Shopping Center in Nederland, Colorado, for the day of the hike. Camping is forbidden along the Niwot Ridge Biosphere Reserve and in the Four Lakes Backcountry Zone within the wilderness, including Long Lake, Lake Isabelle, Isabelle Glacier, Mitchell Lake, Blue Lake, and the trail up Mount Audubon. Within the wilderness are seventeen backcountry camping zones. Caribou, Diamond, Jasper, and Crater Lakes zones have designated campsites. Group size in all backcountry zones is limited to one group up to twelve campers and a limited number of groups numbering one to seven people, depending on the capacity of the zone. Groups of more than twelve people and anything with a motor or engine are prohibited.

Campgrounds outside the wilderness area have some amenities and cost $19 per night. Campgrounds with fewer services cost between $11 and $13 per night. During the summer, these campgrounds typically fill for the weekend by Friday morning. Reservations are available at www.recreation.gov or by calling (877) 444-6777. A nonrefundable charge of for each reserved site is $10.00 for a telephone reservation and $9.00 for a web reservation. Reservations can be made as long as six months in advance and must be made at least 4 days in advance of arrival. However, half the sites in each full-service campground are non reservable and available on a first-come basis. The Forest Service warns of bears in their campgrounds and discourages placing food in a tent.

Trail Finder

Best Hikes for Great Views

1   Meadow and Saint Vrain Mountains
4   Sawtooth Mountain
5   Coney Lake and Upper Coney Lake
9   Lake Isabelle
16 Mount Audubon
15 Blue Lake
20 Diamond Lake
24 South Arapaho Peak
36 Mount Irving Hale
42 Mirror and Crater Lakes
44 Satanta Peak

Best Hikes for Waterfalls

20   Diamond Lake
33 Lost Lake
42 Mirror and Crater Lakes

Best Hikes with Children

6   Brainard Lake
9   Lake Isabelle
15 Blue Lake
33 Lost Lake
45 Columbine Lake

Best Hikes for Wildlife

16 Mount Audubon
29 Woodland Lake
42 Mirror and Crater Lakes

Best Hikes for Photographers

15 Blue Lake
16 Mount Audubon
9   Lake Isabelle
24 South Arapaho Peak
38 Upper Lake
42 Mirror and Crater Lakes
44 Satanta Peak

Best Summit Hikes

Best Hikes for Solitude

Map Legend

══⟨40⟩══	US Highway	■	Building/Point of Interest
══⟨72⟩══	State Highway	⚠	Campground
══[125]══	Local/County Road	⛏	Mine
▬ ▬ ▬ ▬	Featured Trail	▲	Mountain/Summit
▪ ▪ ▪ ▪	Trail	⌣	Pass/Gap
⋯⋯⋯	Off-Trail Hike	○	Town
〜	Small River/Creek	①	Trailhead
⬭	Body of Water		
⬭	Glacier		
▭	National Forest/Park		
▭	Wilderness Area		

East of the Continental Divide

Elk Tooth peeks over ridge above Red Deer Lake.

1 Meadow and Saint Vrain Mountains

This hike at its beginning passes through land cleared by forest fire and now renewing its forest cover. The summits are crowned by alpine tundra.

Start: Saint Vrain Mountain Trailhead

Distance: 9 miles out and back

Hiking time: About 6 hours

Difficulty: Moderate

Trail surface: Dirt

Best season: Summer

Other trail users: Equestrians

Canine compatibility: Dogs are permitted on handheld, 6-foot leashes; slight off-trail detour around a short stretch in and out of Rocky Mountain National Park (if you climb Saint Vrain Mountain)

Fees and permits: None for hiking. Permit required for overnight camping

Trail contacts: USDA Forest Service, Boulder Ranger District, 2140 Yarmouth Ave., Boulder CO 80301; (303) 541-2500; fs.usda.gov/arp

Maps: Trails Illustrated Indian Peaks Gold Hill; USGS Allens Park

Highlights: Alpine tundra, view of Longs Peak, Meadow, and Saint Vrain mountains

Wildlife: Red squirrel, mountain chickadee, pika, white-tailed ptarmigan

Saint Vrain Mountain Trailhead elevation: 8,800 feet

Meadow Mountain elevation: 11,632 feet

Saint Vrain Mountain elevation: 12,162 feet

Finding the trailhead: From CO 7, turn south on Business Rte. 7 into the town of Allenspark, about 17 miles south of Estes Park. Follow Business Rte. 7 to Ski Road. Turn south on Ski Road for 0.4 mile. CR 107E (an alternative route for those coming from Lyons who can turn left onto the other end of Business Rte. 7) joins Ski Road. Continue on Ski Road for 0.9 mile to Roosevelt National Forest. At 0.3 mile inside the national forest is a fork in the road. Take the right-hand fork (FR 116.1) uphill about 0.5 mile to the Saint Vrain Mountain Trailhead. **GPS:** N40° 11' .14"/ W105° 35' .22"

Two circle hikes are possible. One drops from the saddle between Meadow and Saint Vrain mountains along the Rock Creek Trail, which eventually evolves to Rock Creek Road and a junction with a hike back up Forest Service Rd. 116.1 about a half mile to the Saint Vrain Mountain Trailhead. The way down is a maze of elk trails through krummholz, followed by a maze of 4WD tracks outside of the wilderness boundary. If you keep following what seems like the easiest way downhill, Rocky Mountain Search and Rescue will not have to bring out their dogs to find you.

The other circle has rather complicated logistics and is longer but more pleasant. Leave a second vehicle or arrange for transportation at Camp Dick, the beginning of the Middle Saint Vrain Road and (separate) Buchanan Pass Trail. To reach Camp Dick (a Civilian Conservation Corps camp in the 1930s), turn west from CO 72 at Peaceful Valley, 4 miles from the intersection of CO 7 and CO 72 or 9.2 miles north of the town of Ward. On a paved road, drive for a mile through Peaceful Valley

Storm threatens the summit of Saint Vrain Mountain.

Campground to park at the west end of Camp Dick, a mile from CO 72. The 5-mile Middle Saint Vrain Road beyond Camp Dick is a severe trial for high-clearance 4WD vehicles and even for hikers. Therefore, Camp Dick is the end of the road for normal passenger cars.

For 4 miles, the Buchanan Pass Trail passes pleasantly from Camp Dick to the Indian Peaks Wilderness boundary. However, unless you are camped in one of the campgrounds and want to walk from there, it makes no sense to take this trail to Buchanan Pass. Far easier is the trail from Beaver Reservoir (see Hike 3, Buchanan Pass Trail description). From just beyond where the Buchanan Pass Trail crosses the wilderness boundary, the Saint Vrain Mountain Trail climbs precipitously to the right, a way to descend from the mountain, if you have transportation waiting at Camp Dick. GPS: N40° 07' .797"/W105° 31' .45"

Beyond a pleasant start through an aspen grove, the trail winds through a broad area cleared by forest fire for more than 2 miles until it reaches krummholz at tree line. Above the trees, ascend north from the trail to the rounded summit of Meadow Mountain by whatever route seems most convenient. If you have canine hiking companions, do not stray into Rocky Mountain National Park. The top of Meadow Mountain marks the south boundary of the national park, but getting to the top without venturing into the park is fairly simple by avoiding the top of the ridge that leads to the summit. Although the way is very rocky near the top, a multi-flowered alpine meadow covers the summit.

The Saint Vrain Mountain Trail is fairly level as it continues through a blend of krummholz and alpine tundra. A higher rounded hump rising to the southwest is

Bison (buffalo) do not live in Indian Peaks, but their hides and tongue were the basis of business with Indian customers at Saint Vrain trading post on the plains.

SaintVrain Mountain, also on the park boundary, 700 feet above the saddle between Meadow and Saint Vrain. Along the ridge between the two mountains, a boundary changes to make boundary lines conform to natural features coincidentally put a short section of trail within the national park, about 220 yards at its maximum distance from the national forest. The Forest Service tells hikers with dogs not to cross into the national park. To comply with this directive, hikers with leashed dogs (which the Forest Service allows) must detour left at the park boundary.

An off-trail scramble skirts a small promontory that extends east from the ridge between Meadow and Saint Vrain. Try to step on rocks to avoid damage to tundra plants that have not already been sacrificed for a trail. Attempt to stay at the same elevation at which you leave the trail. Return to the trail after it reenters the national forest (still above tree line).

A trail (marked by a pile of rocks) drops from the Saint Vrain Mountain Trail into the valley of Rock Creek. From this intersection is the logical place to leave the trail and ascend right to the top of Saint Vrain. White boundary markers distinguish the national park from the national forest. From the top, you might view other hikers

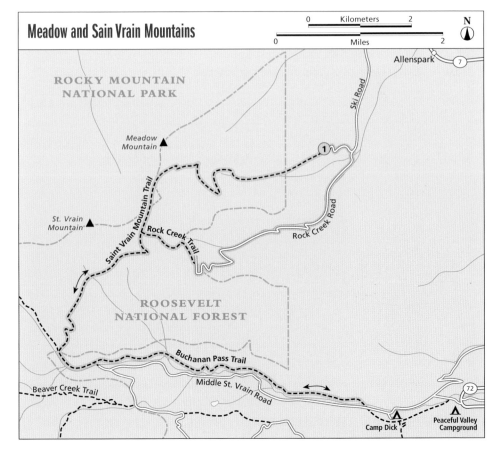

Meadow and Sain Vrain Mountains

panting from the other end of the Saint Vrain Mountain Trail in the Middle Saint Vrain valley. This approach is considerably steeper than hiking from the Allenspark end of the trail. Descending it can lead you eventually out on the Buchanan Pass Trail along Middle Saint Vrain Creek to Camp Dick near Peaceful Valley along CO 72, where, hopefully, you have left a vehicle.

Saint Vrain Mountain is named for the Saint Vrain brothers, major figures in the 1830s and 1840s bison hide trade with various tribes commemorated in Indian Peaks Wilderness. Fort Saint Vrain trading post was about 20 miles east of the mountains at the confluence of Saint Vrain Creek and the South Platte River.

Miles and Directions

0.0   Start at Saint Vrain Mountain Trailhead.

0.7   Cross Indian Peaks Wilderness boundary.

1.5   Pass through final switchback.

2.65 Encounter tree line.

3.15 Trail enters Rocky Mountain National Park.

3.6   Trail exits Rocky Mountain National Park.

3.9   Rock Creek Trail branches to left.

4.45 Reach Saint Vrain Mountain Summit.

8.9   Arrive back at the Saint Vrain Mountain Trailhead.

10.0 Alternatively, return to Camp Dick and second vehicle.

2 Red Deer Lake

Red Deer Lake and Elk Tooth, a distinctive rock formation on the eastern ridge from Ogalalla Peak, are the only natural features named for the area's most prominent herbivore.

Start: Camp Dick
Distance: 13.8 miles out and back
Difficulty: Moderate
Trail surface: Dirt
Best season: Summer
Other trail users: Equestrians
Canine compatibility: Dogs are permitted on 6-foot, handheld leashes
Fees and permits: None for hiking. Permit required for overnight camping

Trail contacts: USDA Forest Service, Boulder Ranger District, 2140 Yarmouth Ave., Boulder CO 80301; (303) 541-2500; fs.usda.gov/arp
Maps: Trails Illustrated Indian Peaks Gold Hill; USGS Allens Park
Highlights: Middle Saint Vrain Creek, wildflowers, Red Deer Lake, view of Elk Tooth
Camp Dick elevation: 8,368 feet
Red Deer Lake elevation: 10,372 feet

Finding the trailhead: To reach Camp Dick, turn west from Colorado Hwy. 72 at Peaceful Valley along paved CR 92, 0.1 mile south of a bridge crossing Middle Saint Vrain Creek. CR 92 is 4.1 miles south of the junction of Colorado Hwy. 72 and Colorado Hwy. 7 or 9.2 miles north of the town of Ward. Follow CR 92 for a mile to an unpaved parking lot at the west end of Camp Dick Campground. **GPS:** N40° 078' .797"/W105° 31' .45"

The Hike

The Buchanan Pass Trail runs in a relaxed fashion along the north side of Middle Saint Vrain Creek to the Indian Peaks Wilderness boundary. Just beyond the boundary, the Saint Vrain Mountain Trail drops through switchbacks to join the Buchanan Pass Trail from the right. The Buchanan Pass Trail continues to parallel the creek to a crossing on a bridge where the Saint Vrain Glacier Trail continues along the north bank. On the south side of Middle Saint Vrain Creek, the Buchanan Pass Trail cuts a broad switchback south, now further from the creek and heading downstream. A fairly gentle grade after 1.1 miles leads to a sharp right turn on the Red Deer Lake trail. Snowfields in early summer melt to water abundant wildflowers. An informal path circles the rock- and krummholz-rimmed shore of Red Deer Lake, a glacier-created tarn, enlarged by a small dam. Circling the shore, a short way left leads to a good view of Elk Tooth.

Miles and Directions

0.0   Start from Camp Dick at the Middle Saint Vrain Trailhead.
4.0   Reach Indian Peaks Wilderness boundary.
4.3   Saint Vrain Mountain Trail descends from the right.

Fireweed provides pink accent to the bank of Middle Saint Vrain Creek.

5.2 Head left across bridge at Buchanan Pass/Saint Vrain Glacier trail junction.

6.3 The spur to Red Deer Lake cuts sharply right from the Buchanan Pass Trail.

6.9 Arrive at Red Deer Lake.

13.8 Arrive back at the Camp Dick.

ELK

Red deer is another name for the same animal that Americans call elk. Native Americans used the increasingly popular name, wapiti. Red Deer Lake occupies an open basin surrounded by rocky glacial debris. The lake's openness near tree line provides a view of Elk Tooth, a promontory rising above a ridge west across the lake and to the right of where a small stream drops into the lake. Elk Tooth sits on the boundary of Indian Peaks Wilderness and Rocky Mountain National Park. It seems appropriate that Elk Tooth and Red Deer Lake are tied visually, for they are the only natural features in Indian Peaks named for one of the region's largest and most prominent wildlife species.

Pioneers in the 1870s saw thousands of elk in this region. As the herds congregated in winter to reach the shelter of lowland meadows, they were shot by market hunters with repeating rifles and hauled to Denver in wagons. There the carcasses yielded three to four cents a pound. By the 1880s and 1890s, namers of natural features saw very few, if any, elk and therefore applied their name to only this lake and a lump on a ridge.

Red deer is an alternative name for elk, especially in England. Some geneticists maintain that the two actually are separate species.

Today, though, elk are abundant again (less so in Indian Peaks Wilderness than in the national park to the north). In 1913, preservation-minded folks in Estes Park provided money to reestablish elk. Elk were shipped by railroad from herds in Montana as far as the town of Lyons, east of Indian Peaks. At Lyons, they were transferred to Stanley Steamer horseless carriages and hauled to Estes Park. The elk were released in the soon-to-be Rocky Mountain National Park, and thrived and spread.

A member of the deer family (like mule deer and moose), elk seem less likely than mule deer to be hit by hikers driving to trailheads. Elk may be less inclined than deer to venture in front of automobiles headed for early starts from trailheads, or perhaps the larger elk are just easier for drivers to spot.

Red Deer Lake

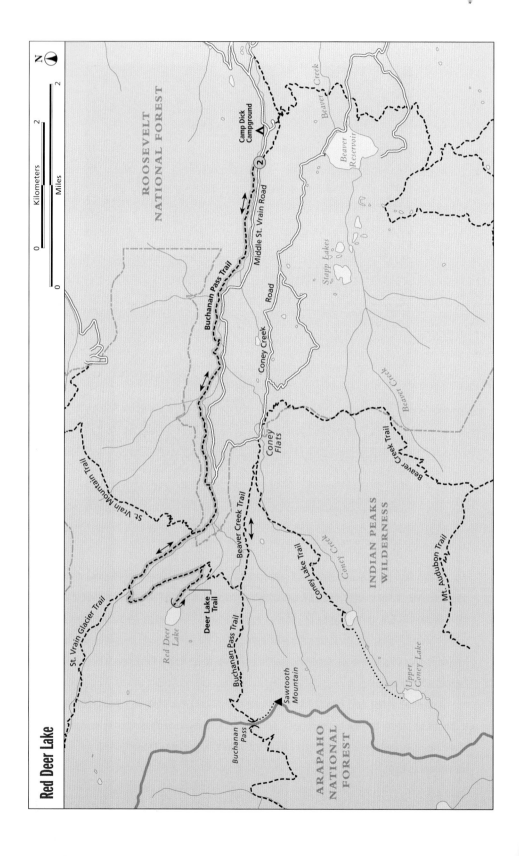

N

Kilometers
0   2
Miles
0   2

ROOSEVELT
NATIONAL FOREST

Beaver Creek

Camp Dick
Campground

2

Middle St. Vrain Road

Beaver
Reservoir

Buchanan Pass Trail

Stapp Lakes

Coney Creek
Road

St. Vrain Mountain Trail

Coney Creek

Coney
Flats

Beaver Creek Trail

Beaver Creek

St. Vrain Glacier Trail

Coney Lake Trail

Beaver Creek Trail

INDIAN PEAKS
WILDERNESS

Red Deer
Lake

Deer Lake
Trail

Coney Creek

Mt. Audubon Trail

Buchanan Pass Trail

Upper
Coney Lake

Sawtooth Mountain

Buchanan
Pass

ARAPAHO
NATIONAL
FOREST

3 Buchanan Pass Trail

The shortest route to Buchanan Pass begins at Beaver Reservoir and leads to a tundra-covered pass below Sawtooth Mountain and over to the western side of Indian Peaks.

Start: North side of Beaver Reservoir
Hiking time: About 8 hours
Distance: 14 miles out and back
Difficulty: Difficult
Trail surface: Rocky 4WD road, followed by dirt
Best season: Summer
Other trail users: 4WD vehicles and equestrians
Canine compatibility: Dogs are permitted on handheld, 6-foot leashes
Fees and permits: None for hiking. Permit required for overnight camping within Indian Peaks Wilderness

Trail contacts: USDA Forest Service, Boulder Ranger District, 2140 Yarmouth Ave., Boulder CO 80301 (303) 541-2515; fs.usda.gov/arp
Maps: Trails Illustrated Indian Peaks Gold Hill; USGS Ward, Allens Park, Isolation Peak
Highlights: Quaking aspen are lovely in September mixed with limber pine; subalpine forest; alpine tundra
Wildlife: Moose in Coney Flats; mule deer, elk, red squirrel, mountain chickadee, pika, brown-capped rosy finch, white-tailed ptarmigan, yellow-bellied marmot
Beaver Reservoir elevation: 9,161 feet
Buchanan Pass elevation: 11,837 feet

Finding the trailhead: To reach Beaver Reservoir, drive 7.4 miles on Colorado Hwy. 72 south of the junction with Colorado Hwy. 7, or 2.5 miles north of the town of Ward. Turn west on gravel CR 96 and drive 2.5 miles, passing a Boy Scout camp, to a roadside parking spot on the north shore of Beaver Reservoir. **GPS:** N40° 12' .276"/W105° 51' .778"

The Hike

The least-lengthy approach to Buchanan Pass begins on the north shore of Beaver Reservoir. (The Buchanan Pass Trail from the Middle Saint Vrain Creek to the north is long; the Buchanan Pass Trail from the west to the pass on the Continental Divide is longer.)

From privately owned Beaver Reservoir, walking up a 4WD road lifts hikers along a comparatively gentle grade through lodgepole pines. Here and there, actual beaver reservoirs built by busy rodents add interest and mosquitoes to this route.

The 3.5-mile road to Coney Flats is filled with large, ankle-twisting rocks that make the route tough for 4WD vehicles, tougher for hikers, and impossible for normal passenger cars. Two miles from Beaver Reservoir, the road divides. The hiking route to the right is somewhat easier on hikers' feet than the vehicle route to the left. But there remain loose rocks exposed by vehicle traffic that used to be permitted on the present walking route.

The hiking route follows a portion of the top of the south wall of the Middle Saint Vrain valley. Forest blocks most of the view into the valley. But, hikers nonetheless feel like they are walking on the edge.

Sawtooth Mountain is easy to distinguish south (left in this photo) of Buchanan Pass along the Continental Divide.

Separated from the bad, bumpy, and bothersome road for more than a mile, hikers meet it again for a thankfully short stretch at a branch of Coney Creek. A bridge (for hikers) crosses the creek to meet the Beaver Creek Trail arriving from the south. A second bridge soon crosses Coney Creek at the end of the 4WD road where hikers encounter the Indian Peaks Wilderness boundary. Here is the Coney Flats Trailhead.

A broad trail leads toward Buchanan Pass, visible as a low saddle marked by a permanent snowfield below the pass to the left. Especially in contrast to walking the 4WD road, this delightful trail is in good shape, passing through limber pine and quaking aspen beyond the trailhead and climbing through subalpine fir and Engelmann spruce. Only 0.2 mile from the Coney Flats Trailhead, the trail to Coney Lake and Upper Coney Lake branches left. As hikers climb toward Buchanan Pass, forest evolves to tundra and tundra to rocks, traversed by switchbacks rising steeply to the pass.

Miles and Directions

0.0	Start at the north side of Beaver Reservoir.
3.4	Hike beyond the Beaver Creek Trail Junction.
3.5	Reach Coney Flats Trailhead.
3.7	Hike beyond the junction of the trail to Coney Lake and Upper Coney Lake.
5.1	Hike beyond the Junction of trail to Red Deer Lake.
7.0	Arrive at Buchanan Pass.
14.0	Return to Beaver Reservoir.
16.1	Alternative, return via Buchanan Pass Trail to Camp Dick.

Buchanan Pass

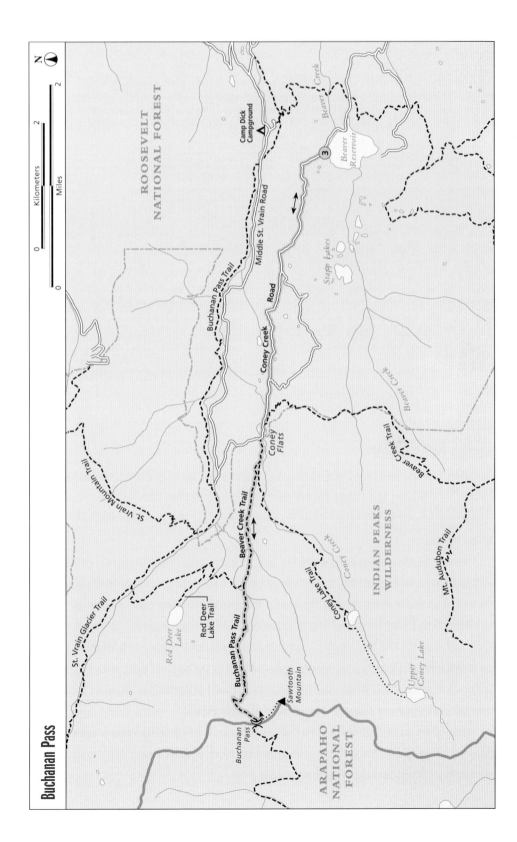

N

0   2   Kilometers
0   2   Miles

ROOSEVELT
NATIONAL FOREST

Beaver Creek

Camp Dick
Campground

3

Beaver
Reservoir

Middle St. Vrain Road

Coney Creek
Road

Stapp Lakes

Buchanan Pass Trail

Beaver Creek

Coney
Flats

St. Vrain Mountain Trail

Beaver Creek Trail

INDIAN PEAKS
WILDERNESS

Beaver Creek Trail

Coney Creek

St. Vrain Glacier Trail

Red Deer
Lake

Red Deer
Lake Trail

Buchanan Pass Trail

Sawtooth Mountain

Buchanan
Pass

Coney Lake Trail

Mt. Audubon Trail

Upper
Coney Lake

ARAPAHO
NATIONAL
FOREST

Beavers are large rodents and excellent engineers, but their ponds along this hike are not as large as human-engineered Beaver Reservoir at the trailhead.

JAMES BUCHANAN

Buchanan Pass and Buchanan Creek presumably commemorate James Buchanan, who, in 1861, was the US President who signed the bill creating Colorado Territory. This was the crowning achievement of what history rightly deems the worst presidential administration suffered by the United States.

Despite significant competition for the title of worst president, Buchanan's status is unlikely to face challenge. Buchanan laid claim to being the worst chief executive by dithering in the face of secession of the South in the quarter year between Abraham Lincoln's election and his taking office. Failing to nip what Buchanan considered to be illegal secession, he handed over to his successor the Civil War, America's worst disaster, made much deadlier by Buchanan's failure to act. Ironically, the worst US president was followed by the best, but there is no memorial to Lincoln in Indian Peaks Wilderness. (The Lincoln Memorial in Washington, DC, does contain Colorado marble quarried a couple of hours south of Indian Peaks.)

Many hikers may be justified to claim that one of the best hikes in Indian Peaks is named for the worst US President. Though "best" is an impossible honor to claim among such a profusion of magnificent hikes, Buchanan Pass is undeniably great.

4 Sawtooth Mountain

Sawtooth Mountain is easy to identify and the farthest east point on the Continental Divide.

Start: North Side of Beaver Reservoir
Hiking time: About 9 hours out and back
Distance: 13 miles
Difficulty: Difficult
Trail surface: Rocky 4WD road and dirt trail
Best season: Summer
Other trail users: 4WD vehicles before wilderness boundary, equestrians
Canine compatibility: Dogs are permitted on 6-foot, handheld leashes
Fees and permits: None for hiking. Permits required for overnight within the Indian Peaks Wilderness

Trail contacts: USDA Forest Service, Boulder Ranger District, 2140 Yarmouth Ave., Boulder CO 80301; (303) 541-2500; fs.usda.gov/arp
Maps: Trails Illustrated Indian Peaks Gold Hill; USGS Ward, Allens Park, Isolation Peak
Highlights: Most eastern point on Continental Divide
Wildlife: Moose in Coney Flats, mule deer, elk, red squirrel, mountain chickadee, pika, brown-capped rosy finch, yellow-bellied marmot
Beaver Reservoir elevation: 9,161 feet Sawtooth Mountain elevation: 12,304 feet

Finding the trailhead: To reach Beaver Reservoir, drive 7.4 miles on Colorado Hwy. 72 south of its junction with Colorado Hwy. 7, or 2.5 miles north of the town of Ward. Turn west on gravel CR 96 and drive 2.5 miles, passing a Boy Scout camp, to a roadside parking spot on the north shore of Beaver Reservoir. **GPS:** N40° 12'.276"/W105 51.778'

The Hike

Aptly named, Sawtooth Mountain is easily identified. From the megalopolis along the eastern base of the Front Range to peaceful, flower-lined trails within the wilderness, the precipitous south-facing side contrasts with a relatively gentler north slope. This silhouette demands conspicuous comparison to the edge of a saw blade. The surrounding peaks are higher but far more abstract in shape than the familiar outline of Sawtooth.

The least-lengthy route to Sawtooth Mountain, the easternmost point on the Continental Divide, begins at Beaver Reservoir and follows the journey to Buchanan Pass (see Hike 3). From a small parking area on the private reservoir's north side, a rocky (even for the Rocky Mountains) 4WD road leads to the Indian Peaks Wilderness boundary at Coney Flats Trailhead. Hikers tend to forget the trials of the initial trail section when they hit the broad, pleasant path west of the trailhead, passing through varied forest types onto the delightful treeless tundra. After a steep grind to Buchanan Pass, a left turn across a half-mile of alpine tundra begins as a clear trail that evaporates among boulders. Surmounting too many boulders and several false summits takes hikers to 467 feet above Buchanan Pass at Sawtooth's flat, geographically unique summit.

Golden banner wildflowers wave below Sawtooth Mountain.

Miles and Directions

0.0   Start at the north side of Beaver Reservoir.

3.4   Arrive at the Beaver Creek Trail Junction.

3.5   Arrive at Coney Flats Trailhead.

3.7   Hike past the junction with the trail to Coney Lake and Upper Coney Lake.

5.1   Hike past the junction of trail to Red Deer Lake.

7.0   Arrive at Buchanan Pass.

7.5   Arrive at the top of Sawtooth Mountain.

15.0 Return to Beaver Reservoir.

16.6 Alternative, return via Buchanan Pass Trail to Camp Dick.

Sawtooth Mountain

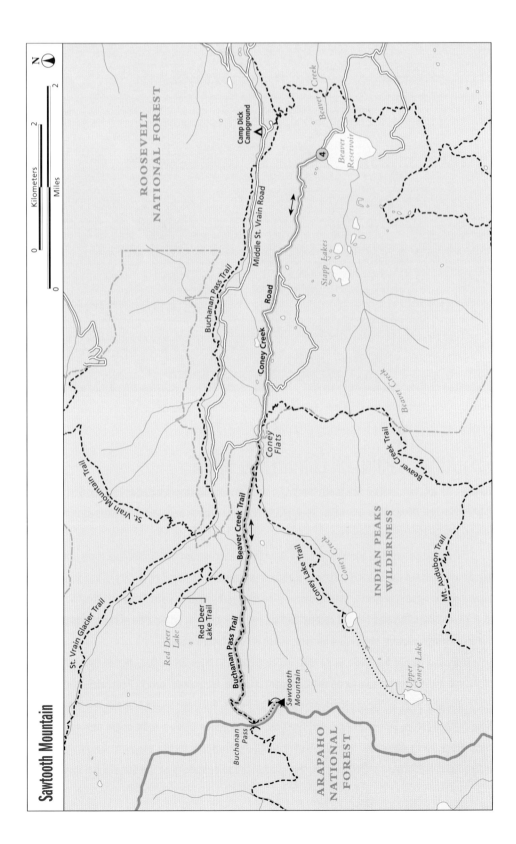

ROOSEVELT
NATIONAL FOREST

Camp Dick
Campground

Beaver Creek

Middle St. Vrain Road

4

Beaver
Reservoir

Coney Creek Road

Stapp Lakes

Buchanan Pass Trail

Coney Flats

Beaver Creek Trail

Beaver Creek

Beaver Creek Trail

St. Vrain Mountain Trail

St. Vrain Glacier Trail

Coney Creek

INDIAN PEAKS
WILDERNESS

Red Deer
Lake

Red Deer
Lake Trail

Coney Lake Trail

Mt. Audubon Trail

Buchanan Pass Trail

Buchanan
Pass

Sawtooth
Mountain

Upper
Coney Lake

ARAPAHO
NATIONAL
FOREST

Kilometers

Miles

N

Yellow-bellied marmots inhabit alpine tundra along the Continental Divide.

EASTERNMOST POINT ON CONTINENTAL DIVIDE

Perhaps its location makes Sawtooth Mountain easy to see. Sawtooth extends further east on the Continental Divide than any other spot, giving it unique status in a land where the direction of water flow is critically important.

The Divide determines whether precipitation flows east toward the Mississippi River drainage or west toward the Colorado River. Because most people in Colorado live east of the Divide, many water diversion projects, spectacular engineering feats, snatch water from wet West Slope to dry East Slope. This has caused conflict among not only folks on either side of the mountains but also among western states and Mexico, which all need more water.

Mountain height has little to do with which direction water flows. Only two of Colorado's fifty-three 14,000-foot peaks sit on the Continental Divide, Grays, and Torreys Peak, visible from South Arapaho Peak in the southern part of Indian Peaks. Between South Arapaho and Mount Neva (named for an individual Arapaho) the Continental Divide takes a right angle turn to the west. From Rocky Mountain National Park's southern boundary to the southern boundary of Indian Peaks Wilderness at Rollins Pass, the spine of the wilderness is on the Continental Divide.

5 Coney Lake and Upper Coney Lake

Coney and Upper Coney lakes, surrounded by masses of rock rubble from icy sculpture, feature piles of stones and natural gardens, perfect habitat for the diminutive, cute critter for which the lakes are named.

Start: Beaver Reservoir
Hiking time: About 10 hours
Distance: 13.8 out and back
Difficulty: Moderate
Trail surface: Rock on 4WD road followed by dirt
Best season: Summer
Other trail users: Equestrians, 4WD vehicles prior to the wilderness boundary
Canine compatibility: Dogs are permitted on 6-foot, handheld leashes
Fees and permits: None for hiking. Permits required for overnight camping within the Indian Peaks Wilderness Area

Trail contacts: USDA Forest Service, Boulder Ranger District, 2140 Yarmouth Ave., Boulder CO 80301; (303) 541-2500; fs.usda.gov/arp
Maps: Trails Illustrated Indian Peaks Gold Hill; USGS Monarch Lake, Ward, Allens Park
Highlights: Coney Lake, Upper Coney Lake
Wildlife: Moose at Coney Flats, mule deer, pika (coney), but not at Coney Flats, which is named for Coney Creek flowing from higher coney habitat
Beaver Reservoir elevation: 9,161 feet
Upper Coney Lake elevation: 10,940 feet

Finding the trailhead: To reach Beaver Reservoir, drive 7.4 miles on Colorado Hwy. 72 south of its junction with Colorado Hwy. 7 or 2.5 miles north of the town of Ward. Turn west on CR 96 and drive 2.5 miles, passing a Boy Scout camp, to a roadside parking spot on the north shore of Beaver Reservoir. **GPS:** N40° 12' .276"/W105° 51' .778"

The Hike

To reach the Coney Creek Trail and the lakes of the same name from Beaver Reservoir, begin by hiking up National Forest System Road (NFSR) 507. This road to Coney Flats is described by the Forest Service as "a rocky, 4WD EXTREME route for experienced drivers only with a high clearance 4WD vehicle." This description is generous. The road is tough for 4WD vehicles, tougher for hikers, and impossible for normal passenger cars. The large rocks kicked up by 4WD vehicles are hard on booted feet. Two miles from Beaver Reservoir, the road divides: vehicles to the left, hikers to the right. This gives hikers some respite, but the rocks exposed when this trail was also open to 4WD, although less likely to roll under hikers' feet, still make for rough going. After a bit more than a mile, the walking trail rejoins the 4WD road at a branch of Coney Creek, for a thankfully short stretch past two bridged crossings of the creek to reach the end of the 4WD road and the wilderness boundary at Coney Flats Trailhead.

The Coney Creek Trail heads left 0.2 mile inside the wilderness boundary, paralleling the Beaver Creek Trail (which heads toward Buchanan Pass) through a meadow to a bridgeless crossing of Coney Creek. Following a somewhat steeper grade, the

The rock rubble around Upper Coney Lake provides shelter to coneys.

trail benefits from forest shade along Coney Creek. The path bends right to circle a small pond before climbing steeply up a narrow valley to Coney Lake.

No maintained trail links Coney Lake and Upper Coney Lake. Follow the Coney Creek drainage through loose rocks and willows for a mile to Upper Coney Lake.

Miles and Directions

0.0   Start at Beaver Reservoir.

3.4   Arrive at Coney Flats Trailhead.

3.6   Bear left on Coney Creek Trail.

3.85 Ford Coney Creek to continue on the trail on the other bank.

5.2   Circle right around pond.

5.9   View Coney Lake at tree line.

6.9   Arrive at Upper Coney Lake.

13.8 Arrive back at Beaver Reservoir.

Noble, but failed, attempts to improve on the King James Bible translation of Proverbs 30:26 describe badgers as "feeble folk," which this badger evidently finds amusing (or insulting).

A coney harvests tundra plants to dry as hay for winter food.

CONEYS

Coney Lake and Upper Coney Lake provide homes for coney colonies. These 6-inch-long rabbit relatives that resemble quick, gray-furred potatoes with round ears shelter and store hay in niches among piles of rocks fallen from the cliffs above. Nearby are alpine meadows where these incredibly cute creatures harvest flowers, grass, and sedges to dry for winter food.

The King James translation of Proverbs 30:26 from Old Testament Hebrew admires the wisdom of conies, which it says, "are a feeble folk, yet make their homes in the rocks." Later English translations tend to be far less accurate, substituting badgers for conies. Badgers are fierce, large weasels, not the least feeble and living in nonrocky meadows, where digging for rodents to eat is easy. However, the King James, although better from a natural history standpoint, is not precisely accurate in its identification. The original Hebrew name is *shafan*, today known as a rock hyrax. The translators serving the first Stewart King of England knew no more about hyraxes than do the typical Indian Peaks hikers and threw in coney, a name for rabbit.

Nineteenth-century explorers of European ancestry noticed, when they reached the heights of the Rockies, loud, sharp, shrill warning squeaks of critters rather like round-eared rabbits with no visible tails. Some of these explorers might have been familiar with a New York island named for its large rabbit population (to be followed eventually by a famous amusement park). But they for sure were familiar with King James natural history. These cute North American rock dwellers seemed to be what their Bible called coneys. Although coneys and hyraxes are not related, they do seem similar due to the process of converging evolution to which these explorers had not been introduced.

Subsequent zoologists adopted the name of pika for this rabbit relative, using a Mongol word for a very similar species inhabiting Asian mountains (yes, really). Meanwhile, namers of natural features in Indian Peaks were busy inking coney on maps. Other namers used Cony Creek, Cony Lake, and Cony Pass one valley north in Rocky Mountain National Park. The "e" commonly is dropped today, and cony is as commonly used as pika. To further the humorous confusion, sometimes pika is pronounced *pieka* and sometimes *peeka*.

Unfortunately, today pika face a far more serious tragedy brought on by global warming. Evolved to make hay on the cold heights, pika can die easily from overheating. Thus, they are as vulnerable to the greenhouse effect as are polar bears. Already living at high altitude, pika often have no higher, cooler place to go. Although the charming rock rabbits around Coney and Upper Coney lakes likely can hide successfully from killing heat, zoologists in Nevada mountains report that pika already have died out in some of their former, now warmer, habitats. Happily, hikers striving to find the least difficult way from Coney Lake to dramatic Upper Coney Lake certainly will hear coney calls. These should not be interpreted as suggesting the best route.

Coney Lake

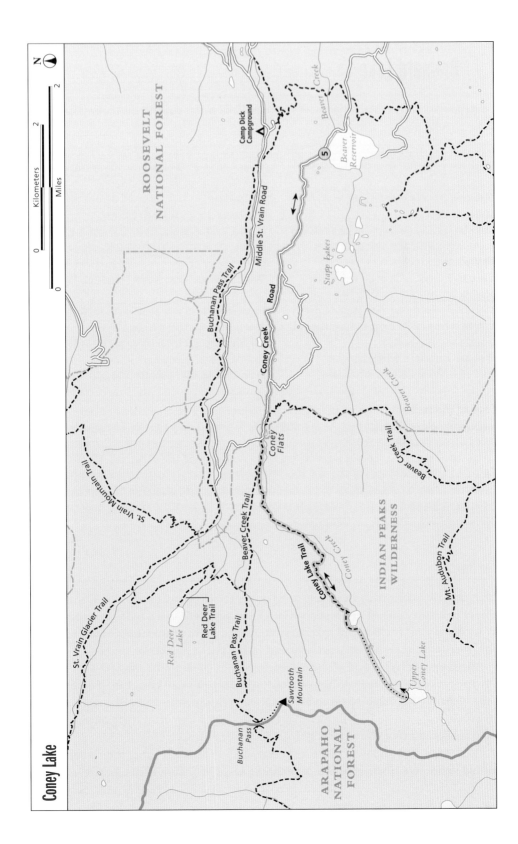

N

Kilometers
0   2

Miles
0   2

ROOSEVELT NATIONAL FOREST

Beaver Creek

Camp Dick Campground

Middle St. Vrain Road

5

Beaver Reservoir

Coney Creek Road

Coney Creek

Stapp Lakes

Buchanan Pass Trail

St. Vrain Mountain Trail

Coney Flats

Beaver Creek Trail

St. Vrain Glacier Trail

Beaver Creek Trail

Red Deer Lake

Red Deer Lake Trail

Buchanan Pass Trail

Coney Lake Trail

Coney Creek

INDIAN PEAKS WILDERNESS

Mt. Audubon Trail

Sawtooth Mountain

Buchanan Pass

ARAPAHO NATIONAL FOREST

Upper Coney Lake

6 Brainard Lake

Although not within the wilderness, Brainard Lake is the gateway to Indian Peaks' most popular trails.

Start: Niwot Picnic Area on the west end of Brainard Lake
Distance: 0.8 mile out and back
Difficulty: Easy
Trail surface: Dirt (and asphalt for those who chose to go all the way around the lake)
Best season: Summer
Other trail users: Pedestrians only on the south shore; bicyclists on the paved north shore road (now closed to automobile traffic)
Canine compatibility: Dogs are permitted on 6-foot, handheld leashes
Fees and Permits: A vehicle fee good for 3 days provides access to trailheads located within the Brainard Lake Recreation Area. Camping allowed only at Pawnee Campground
Trail contacts: USDA Forest Service, Boulder Ranger District, 2140 Yarmouth Ave., Boulder CO 80301; (303) 541-2500; fs.usda.gov/arp
Maps: Trails Illustrated Indian Peaks Gold Hill; USGS Allens Park
Highlights: Broad view of Indian Peaks Wilderness from east end of the lake.
Wildlife: Moose, mule deer, white-crowned sparrow, Wilson's warbler
Brainard Lake level elevation: 10,360 feet

Finding the trailhead: To reach trailheads in the Brainard Lake area, drive to the historic mining town of Ward on Colorado Hwy. 72. Just north of Ward, turn west at a sign that indicates the paved Brainard Lake Road to Brainard Lake Recreation Area. A fee collection booth is 2.7 miles up the road. Less than a half mile further is Red Rock Lake on the left side of the road. The lake presents a good view of Indian Peaks and water lilies covering the lake's surface. You will not see water lilies further on. You might see moose feeding in the lake, a sight often seen by hikers on the trails ahead. Brainard Lake is 1.7 miles beyond Red Rock Lake. Proceed 0.4 miles to the west end of the lake at Niwot Picnic Area. **GPS:** N40° 5' .22"/W105° 38' .11"

The Hike

Brainard Lake is formed by a concrete dam built by the Civilian Conservation Corps as part of an unsuccessful effort to end the Great Depression. The lake is not within Indian Peaks Wilderness. The Brainard Lake Recreation Area is east of wilderness boundaries. Brainard Lake is the wilderness gateway used by the largest number of visitors.

However, perhaps not all of these visitors want to climb to the top of Navajo or Pawnee peaks. Perhaps they do not even care to circumambulate Long Lake. For these folks, there is a flat, often broad and smooth trail following the south Brainard Lake shoreline. It appears to be a former roadway abandoned after road realignment and now being naturally restored by willows, alders, and spruces.

The alders and willows comprise moose salad. Pedestrians along the shoreline should notice in trailside grass the depressions caused by moose sleeping there—big

Brainard Lake reflects evening light.

areas of bent down grass to rest a cow and much smaller depressions for two calves. Also visible in the trail are vaguely heart-shaped moose tracks together with much smaller mule deer hoof prints.

Broad willow flats provide food and cover for moose as well as shelter for various bird species. Most numerous and obvious birds are white-crowned sparrows with flashy white-and-black stripes on the heads of mature birds and unending, cheeping calls. Smaller, but even more dramatic, are Wilson's warblers with yellow and olive bodies and black skullcaps. Other birds include familiar robins, ravens soaring overhead, and broad-tailed hummingbirds, the males easily identified by the whining whistle made by slots in their wings. Near the west end of the lake, a shallow stream adds its pleasant babble to the bird harmony, but in early July, it can be a challenge to cross the 10-foot-wide flow across the trail.

Flowers along this nature stroll include the woody shrub, bushy cinquefoil, and blooming yellow throughout the summer. Other flowers that bloom once are yellow paintbrush, bistort, goldenrod, fireweed, and harebell. Alien clover arrived decades ago when horses that had been eating clover dropped its seeds well fertilized in feces. Yarrow is a common but inconspicuous white flower with fern-like leaves that inspired another name, chipmunk tails. Yarrow has been used for millennia to cure nearly any ailment. Sometimes it works.

Yarrow's scientific genus name is *Achillae* because the legendary Greek hero Achilles was said to have treated his soldiers' wounds with a yarrow poultice. It sooths mucous membranes, slows the flow of blood, and dulls pain. Utes called it wound

Monkshood beauty disguises its poison.

medicine, and their Euro–American successors labeled it nosebleed plant. Indian heal-
ers discouraged habitual use, which could damage mucous membranes. It is safer to
treat pain with aspirin from a bottle, originally developed by pharmacologists from
willow bark, similar to that seen south of Brainard Lake.

Yarrow to the uneducated eye might resemble water hemlock, which also has
masses of small, white blossoms growing in clumps at the top of the plant. Water
hemlock is one of the most famous poisons because the Greek philosopher Socrates
was executed by being ordered to drink a deadly hemlock brew. A more easily iden-
tifiable and beautiful poisonous plant is monkshood, blooming around the lake. Its
blossoms resemble the hood on a traditional monk's garment, normally dark purple,

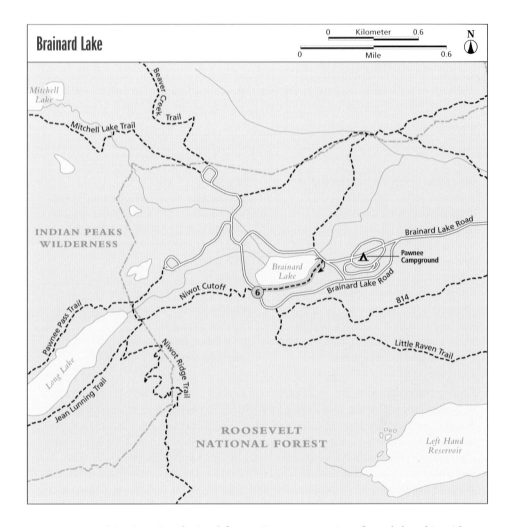

Brainard Lake

0 — Kilometer — 0.6   N

0 — Mile — 0.6

Mitchell Lake

Beaver Creek Trail

Mitchell Lake Trail

INDIAN PEAKS WILDERNESS

Brainard Lake Road

Pawnee Campground

Brainard Lake

Niwot Cutoff

6

Brainard Lake Road

814

Pawnee Pass Trail

Niwot Ridge Trail

Long Lake

Little Raven Trail

Jean Lunning Trail

ROOSEVELT NATIONAL FOREST

Left Hand Reservoir

sometimes white. Aconite obtained from a European species of monkshood is said to have been the favorite poison used during the Italian Renaissance by Lucrezia Borgia to eliminate political rivals.

From the east end of Brainard Lake, it is easy, albeit somewhat less interesting, to cross the dam and return to Niwot Picnic Area via a paved bike path (old road) that follows the northern shore. On this side, willow is far less common. Mature forest of Engelmann spruce and subalpine fir is varied somewhat by occasional limber and lodgepole pines.

Miles and Directions

0.0   Head east to Brainard Lake at Niwot Picnic Area.

0.1   Encounter a shallow stream flowing across path.

0.4   View broad Indian Peaks vista from the east end of lake.

0.8   Arrive back at Niwot Picnic Area (alternative return along bike path on north shore adds about 0.2 mile).

7 Niwot Cutoff Trail

More than a shortcut to Long Lake when parking at higher trailheads is full, the Niwot Cutoff is a peaceful route through magnificent subalpine forest to even more magnificent subalpine meadow flowers.

Start: Niwot Picnic Area
Hiking time: About 1 hour, assuming no pauses for natural distractions
Distance: One mile out and back
Difficulty: Easy
Trail surface: Dirt
Best season: Summer
Other trail users: Pedestrians only
Canine compatibility: Dogs are permitted on handheld, 6-foot leashes
Fees and permits: A vehicle fee good for 3 days provides access to trailheads located in Brainard Lake Recreation Area.

Camping prohibited except in Pawnee Campground
Trail contacts: USDA Forest Service, Boulder Ranger District, 2140 Yarmouth Ave., Boulder CO 80301; (303) 541-2500; fs.usda.gov/arp
Maps: Trails Illustrated Indian Peaks Gold Hill; USGS Ward
Highlights: Subalpine forest and meadow, broad view of Indian Peaks from Long Lake
Wildlife: Moose, mule deer, red squirrel, mountain chickadee
Niwot Picnic Area elevation: 10,360 feet
Long Lake elevation: 10,521 feet

Finding the trailhead: To reach trailheads in the Brainard Lake area, drive to the historic mining town of Ward on Colorado Hwy. 72. Just north of Ward, turn west where a sign indicates paved Brainard Lake Road to Brainard Lake Recreation Area. A fee collection booth is 2.7 miles up the road. Less than a half mile further is Red Rock Lake on the left side of the road. The lake presents a good view of Indian Peaks and water lilies covering the lake's surface. You will not see water lilies further on. You might see moose feeding in the lake, a sight often seen by hikers on the trails ahead. Brainard Lake is 1.7 miles beyond Red Rock Lake. Proceed 0.4 mile to the west end of the lake at Niwot Picnic Area. **GPS:** N40° 5' .22"/W105° 38' .11"

The Hike

The most common greeting when encountering another hiker on the Niwot Cutoff Trail is not "Hi," or "Hello," or "Howdy." Rather, hikers here frequently say, "Seen any moose?" When researching this trail, I kept track of how many hikers greeted me with, "Seen any moose?" It was 80 percent. The trend became so pervasive that when a woman greeted me with "Good morning," I actually asked her why she had not asked if I had seen any moose. So she obligingly asked, "Seen any moose?" I had not on that day, but she had the previous day on the trail to Blue Lake. I did not include her in the 80 percent.

Most hikers on this trail climb it because they cannot find, or just correctly assume that they cannot find parking at the trailheads above. Early arrival for trailhead parking is essential on a July or early August weekend. Indeed, early arrival is necessary

Yellow composites contrast with red Indian paintbrush wildflowers at Long Lake.

even at the picnic area parking at the west end of Brainard Lake, the base of the Niwot Cutoff Trail.

Certainly, this cutoff path is not a sacrificial walk. The trail ascends through glorious and mature subalpine forest of Engelmann spruce and subalpine fir. Light blue Jacob's ladder wildflowers border the sunny trail edge.

Then the forest opens to sunny, subalpine meadow filled with elephants. These elephants are spikes of little red elephant wildflowers, each dark pink bloom looking obviously like an elephant's head. The elephant herd blends with a wild array of other bright floral colors, most likely at its height in mid to late July. Yellow composites mix with red paintbrush, pink queen's crown, and blue harebell below the rock-blanketed flank of Mount Audubon rising to the north above musical South Saint Vrain Creek.

The trail ends at grassy excavation pits with abandoned buckets of earth-moving machines that scooped subalpine glory into the creek to flood willow wetlands that would have been ideal moose habitat. However, at the time Long Lake became a reservoir, moose had not yet been imported from Utah and Wyoming to participate in a rather recent population boom.

Miles and Directions

0.0   Leave Niwot Picnic Area.

0.25   Forest transitions to wildflower meadow.

0.5   Arrive at Long Lake.

1.0   Arrive back at the Niwot Picnic Area.

Fireweed seeds carry wildflower glory at Long Lake into fall.

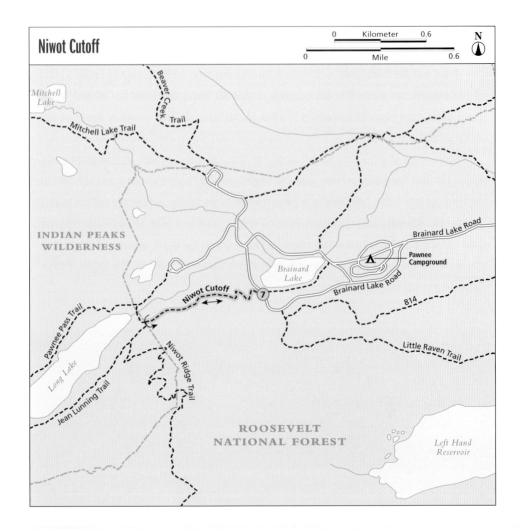

0   Kilometer   0.6

N

0   Mile   0.6

Mitchell Lake

Beaver Creek Trail

Mitchell Lake Trail

INDIAN PEAKS WILDERNESS

Brainard Lake Road

Pawnee Campground

Brainard Lake

Niwot Cutoff

7

Brainard Lake Road

814

Pawnee Pass Trail

Long Lake

Niwot Ridge Trail

Jean Lunning Trail

Little Raven Trail

ROOSEVELT NATIONAL FOREST

Left Hand Reservoir

NIWOT

Niwot Cutoff is one way to reach Niwot Ridge, a center of tundra research outside wilderness boundaries. Niwot was a prominent Arapaho warrior who supposedly was killed in the Sand Creek Massacre in eastern Colorado in 1864. In fact, he survived to participate in the war generated by that infamous attack on a peaceful Cheyenne village harboring allied Arapahos. Four years later, Niwot evidently was present in a Cheyenne village along the Washita River in Oklahoma when it was attacked by Lt. Col. George Custer, who tracked hostile Indians there from a raid in Kansas. Custer rescued two of the three white women he was trying to retrieve. The third was killed.

Custer also lost (reputedly to Indians led by Niwot) a detachment of twenty troopers led by Major Joel Elliot, a loss which cost Custer considerable prestige. This embarrassing loss contributed to Custer's fatal decisions in attacking a large gathering of hostile horse-nomads in 1876 along the Little Bighorn River in Montana.

Niwot was the main leader of the southern Arapahos from 1889 through the early 1900s, after which his son followed in his footsteps. Eventually, Niwot converted to Christianity and spoke of his experiences to gatherings of other Christians in the first decade of the twentieth century. He died in 1911.

Niwot is the Arapaho word for left hand. One photo of Niwot (he was photographed often) shows his right hand with severely mangled fingers, possibly from sun dance participation, or accident, or war. Today, Left Hand is a name applied to uncounted businesses and landmarks in Colorado. However, because history never is simple, there is a point of confusion resulting from the naming of Niwot Mountain above Left Hand Creek. The creek was named long before the mountain and likely before Niwot was born. A well-known fur trader in the 1830s, William Sublette, was left-handed, and the creek was named for him.

"Seen any moose?"

8 Long Lake Loop

Long Lake obviously is named for its shape, but it also is long on delights.

Start: Long Lake Trailhead
Hiking time: About 2 hours
Distance: 2.7-mile loop
Difficulty: Easy
Trail surface: Dirt
Best season: Summer
Other trail users: Hikers only
Canine compatibility: Dogs are permitted on handheld, 6-foot leash
Fees and permits: A vehicle fee good for 3 days provides access to trailheads located in Brainard Lake Recreation Area. Camping prohibited

Trail contacts: USDA Forest Service, Boulder Ranger District, 2140 Yarmouth Ave., Boulder CO 80301; (303) 541-2500; fs.usda.gov/arp
Maps: Trails Illustrated Indian Peaks Gold Hill; USGS Allens Park
Highlights: Wildflowers, broad view of Indian Peaks from the east end
Wildlife: Moose, mule deer, red squirrel, mountain chickadee
Long Lake Trailhead elevation: 10,480 feet
Long Lake elevation: 10,521 feet

Finding the trailhead: To reach trailheads in the Brainard Lake area, drive to the historic mining town of Ward on Colorado Hwy. 72. Just north of Ward, turn west on Brainard Lake Road at a sign that indicates the paved road to Brainard Lake Recreation Area. A fee collection booth is 2.7 miles up the road. Less than a half mile further is Red Rock Lake, on the left side of the road. The lake presents a good view of Indian Peaks and water lilies covering the lake's surface. You will not see water lilies further on. You might see moose feeding by the lake, a sight often seen by hikers on the trails ahead. Brainard Lake is 1.7 miles beyond Red Rock Lake. Drive west of Brainard Lake to a split in the road with the Mitchell Creek and Beaver Creek Trailheads to the right and Long Lake Trailhead for the Pawnee Pass Trail to the left. **GPS:** N40° 04' .674"/W105° 35' .077"

The Hike

A pleasant, easy walk through subalpine forest leads after 0.2 mile to a trail junction at Long Lake. If you are headed to a higher destination, you can speed things along by following the shorter way along the right (north) side of the lake.

The Jean Lunning Trail to the left, at the lake's east end just within the wilderness boundary, loops around the lake through lovely subalpine forests and meadows, bridging marshes where hikers might see moose. It is an easy and charming circuit named for a congressional staffer who shepherded the bill creating Indian Peaks Wilderness through the legislative process.

An easy hike seems to suggest a convenient, late-morning start. This would be a mistake both for convenience and aesthetic enjoyment. Understandably, the trailhead parking lot fills early. Alternative parking areas are progressively further east as far as a large lot east of Brainard Lake.

Long Lake is a short, easy hike from its trailhead.

Beginning the hike early enough to find trailhead parking also brings early rising hikers to Long Lake at the normally prettiest time of day. This rule has some exception in autumn, when gold and red lakeside shrubs display vibrant color as the sun shines through the leaves from the southwest in the afternoon, setting them aglow with a stained-glass window effect.

Hikers with the opportunity for early arrival are blessed by a reduced chance of wind. When the sun has not had time to heat the day's atmosphere and stir convection currents in the air all lakes are more likely to be still and mirror the surrounding peaks. This doubling of visual wonder at sunrise is particularly impressive on the east side of Indian Peaks, where the low angle of the sun's rays have to pass through a longer span of atmosphere that filters out cooler light while allowing the warmer colored end of the spectrum to reflect from lakes and peaks, or just from peaks if contrary weather causes wind to ruffle the water.

Of course, a sunrise start only increases the odds for (but does not guarantee) a reflection view. Jesus is quoted as observing that the wind blows wherever it wishes, and you do not know where it comes from or where it goes (*John* 3:8). Even if an instrument installed atop Niwot Ridge (reached by an unsigned trail climbing left from the Jean Lunning Trail on the south side of Long Lake) records wind data, no scientist monitoring that data for the Institute of Arctic and Alpine Research is going to assure a perfect reflection photo on any given day.

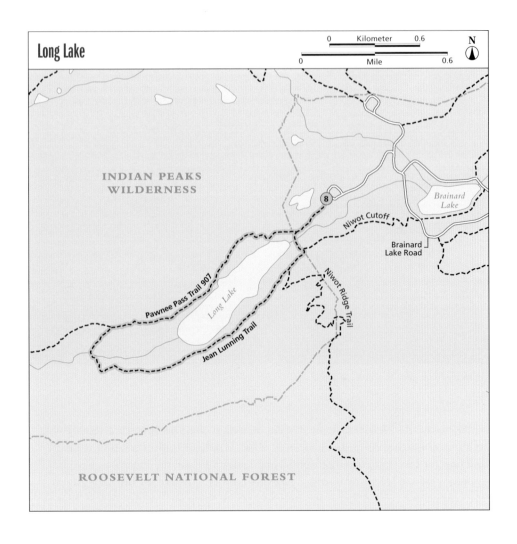

Long Lake

INDIAN PEAKS
WILDERNESS

Brainard
Lake

8

Niwot Cutoff

Brainard
Lake Road

Pawnee Pass Trail 907

Long Lake

Niwot Ridge Trail

Jean Lunning Trail

ROOSEVELT NATIONAL FOREST

0   Kilometer   0.6

0   Mile   0.6

N

Autumn leaves color the edge of Long Lake.

Poetically, the New Testament (Greek) as well as the Old Testament (Hebrew) both use words that mean simultaneously wind, breath, or spirit. Perhaps it is more satisfying for hikers circumambulating Long Lake to follow the biblical policy and consider pleasant breeze or howling gale that both are possible on the same day as representing spirit. Wind shapes the lakes and plants. Spirit, such as that of Jean Lunning pushing for legal protection of the wilderness or of hundreds of volunteers who give their time to help visitors and instruct about wilderness preservation, shapes hikers' opportunities to enjoy Indian Peaks trails.

Miles and Directions

0.0   Start at Long Lake Trailhead.

0.2   Reach Long Lake and head left on Jean Lunning Trail.

1.5   Jean Lunning Trail meets Pawnee Pass Trail beyond west end of lake; turn right.

2.7   Arrive back at the Long Lake Trailhead.

9 Lake Isabelle

Lake Isabelle may be the most popular hike in Indian Peaks and is one of the prettiest lakes in Colorado—except when it is not.

Start: Long Lake Trailhead
Hiking time: About 3 hours
Distance: 4.2 miles out and back
Difficulty: Easy
Trail surface: Dirt
Best season: Summer
Other trail users: Hikers only.
Canine compatibility: Dogs are permitted with handheld, 6-foot leashes.
Fees and permits: A vehicle fee good for 3 days provides access to trailheads located in the Brainard Lake Recreation Area.
Camping is prohibited except at Pawnee Campground.
Trail contacts: USDS Forest Service, Boulder Ranger District, 2140 Yarmouth Ave., Boulder CO 80301; (303) 541-2500; fs.usda.gov/arp
Maps: Trails Illustrated Indian Peaks Gold Hill; USGS Ward
Highlights: Long Lake, Lake Isabelle
Wildlife: Moose, mule deer, red squirrel, gray jay, mountain chickadee
Long Lake Trailhead elevation: 10,480 feet
Lake Isabelle elevation: 10,868 feet

Finding the trailhead: To reach trailheads in Brainard Lake Recreation Area, drive to the historic mining town of Ward on Colorado Hwy. 72. Just north of Ward, turn west on paved Brainard Lake Road to Brainard Lake Recreation Area. A fee collection booth is 2.7 miles up the road. Less than a half mile further is Red Rock Lake on the left side of the road. The lake presents a good view of Indian Peaks and water lilies covering the lake's surface. You will not see water lilies further on. You might see moose feeding by the lake, a sight often enjoyed by hikers on the trails ahead. Brainard Lake is 1.7 miles beyond Red Rock Lake. Proceed around the south shore to a fork in the road beyond the lake's west end. Right leads to Mitchell Lake and Beaver Creek trailheads. Left leads to Long Lake Trailhead and the Pawnee Pass Trail to Lake Isabelle. **GPS:** N40° 04' .674"/ W105° 35' .007"

The Hike

Lake Isabelle glimmers with Maroon Lake in White River National Forest, Dream Lake in Rocky Mountain National Park, and Mirror Lake on the West Slope of Indian Peaks as one of the prettiest lakes in Colorado. Except when it does not.

At the height of the hiking season in late July or early August, Lake Isabelle is drained to supply water to the thirsty plains. Water use is a very big deal in dry Colorado with the Ogallala Aquifer growing ever less able to supply higher amounts of water for an ever-increasing population to pump for drinking, bathing, irrigating, flushing, and fracking for fuel. In this damp struggle, the aesthetic concerns of hikers do not count for much especially because utilitarian water use began long before anyone suggested the Wilderness Act of 1964.

Alpenglow reflects from Navajo and Apache peaks above Lake Isabelle.

Indian paintbrush decorae slopes above Lake Isabelle.

Prepared for possible disappointment in missing one of Colorado's most spectacular vistas at Lake Isabelle during half the summer and all of the fall, hikers can be certain of abundant natural rewards along the trail below the lake. No woodland in Colorado is more beautiful than the subalpine forest extending along the Pawnee Pass Trail for most of the easy 2.1 miles to Isabelle. Spectacular wildflower displays color meadows at both ends of the trail while Long Lake glimmers through the trees. Dramatic mountains, particularly Navajo Peak, rake across the sky above the trail. Lake Isabelle was named for Isabelle Glacier, reached by a trail around the right (north) lakeshore. Junius Henderson, a science faculty member at Colorado University named the glacier for fellow Boulder resident Isabelle Fair. A previous, more descriptive name was Timberline Lake.

Miles and Directions

0.0   Start at Long Lake Trailhead.
0.2   Pawnee Pass Trail meets the Jean Lunning Trail, which circles Long Lake to the left.
1.2   Jean Lunning Trail rejoins Pawnee Pass Trail.
2.1   Pawnee Pass Trail climbs to the right just short of Isabelle Lake.
4.2   Arrive back at the Long Lake Trailhead.

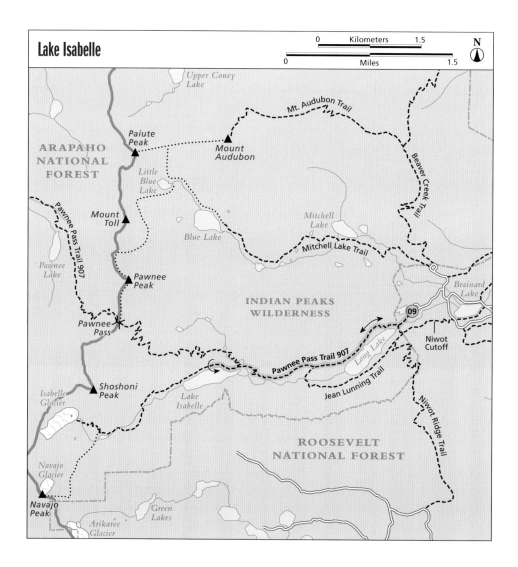

Lake Isabelle

Kilometers 0 — 1.5
Miles 0 — 1.5

N

Upper Coney Lake

Mt. Audubon Trail

Paiute Peak

ARAPAHO NATIONAL FOREST

Mount Audubon

Little Blue Lake

Mitchell Lake

Mount Toll

Blue Lake

Beaver Creek Trail

Mitchell Lake Trail

Brainard Lake

Pawnee Pass Trail 907

Pawnee Lake

Pawnee Peak

INDIAN PEAKS WILDERNESS

09

Pawnee Pass

Long Lake

Niwot Cutoff

Pawnee Pass Trail 907

Isabelle Glacier

Shoshoni Peak

Lake Isabelle

Jean Lunning Trail

Niwot Ridge Trail

Navajo Glacier

ROOSEVELT NATIONAL FOREST

Navajo Peak

Green Lakes

Arikaree Glacier

10 Navajo Peak

Heirloom silver and turquoise jewelry, finely woven wool blankets, herds of sheep, and dramatic (non-Colorado) buttes form the core of American western movies. Navajo is a label easy to remember.

Start: Long Lake Trailhead
Hiking time: About 12 hours
Distance: 6.25 miles
Difficulty: Difficult
Trail surface: Dirt and loose rock (scree)
Best season: Summer
Other trail users: Hikers only
Canine compatibility: Dogs are permitted on handheld, 6-foot leashes, but the last climb to the top is not suitable for dogs because they lack the grasping thumbs that humans find so useful in scaling the summit
Fees and permits: A vehicle fee good for 3 days provides access to the trailheads

located in Brainard Lake Recreation Area. Camping is prohibited except in the Pawnee Campground
Trail contacts: USDA Forest Service, Boulder Ranger District, 2140 Yarmouth Ave., Boulder CO 80301; (303) 541-2500; fs.usda.gov/arp
Maps: Trails Illustrated Indian Peaks Gold Hill; USGS Ward, Monarch Lake
Highlights: Long Lake, Lake Isabelle, airplane gully wreckage, Navajo Peak summit
Wildlife: Moose, mule deer, red squirrel, gray jay, mountain chickadee, pika
Long Lake Trailhead: 10,480 feet
Navajo Peak: 13,409 feet

Finding the trailhead: To reach trailheads in the Brainard Lake area, drive to the historic mining town of Ward on Colorado Hwy. 72. Just north of Ward, turn west on paved Brainard Lake Road to Brainard Lake Recreation Area. A fee collection booth is 2.7 miles up the road. Less than a half mile further is Red Rock Lake on the left side of the road. Do not look for the moose that might be feeding among the lily pads because you do not have time to stop. Brainard Lake is 1.7 miles beyond Red Rock Lake. Drive beyond the west end of Brainard Lake to a split in the road. Bear left to Long Lake Trailhead. **GPS:** N40° 04' .674"/W105° 35' .077"

The Hike

Uniquely, Navajo Peak's conical shape looks much the same from every direction. Hikers can see their goal for most of the route. Beginning at Long Lake Trailhead, follow the Pawnee Pass Trail to the right at Long Lake (see Long Lake Loop and Lake Isabelle hikes, 8 and 9). After less than two miles of easy strolling through lovely woods, switchbacks lift the trail to the level of an alpine meadow accented by a flower-lined brook. Beyond the stream ford, Lake Isabelle is on the left, hidden by a low ridge. Here is the first patch of snow; there will be more.

Above the lake, the long ridge rising from behind and to the left is Niwot Ridge. Navajo is the conical peak. To the right of Navajo is double-humped Apache Peak with Shoshoni Peak on the far right. On the northeastern flank of Apache to the left

Airplane wreckage is scattered in Airplane Gully on the flank of Navajo Peak.

of Shoshoni is Isabelle Glacier. A path along the northern shore of Isabelle Lake heads toward the glacier, but on the way to Navajo, you leave the path before it reaches the glacier.

On the glacier-cut ledges above Isabelle Lake, the trail passes tundra meadows along South Saint Vrain Creek, much diminished in size near its source in the glacier. At a small, cliff-bordered lake, unnamed by the US Geological Survey but called Isabelle Tarn by some hikers, leave the trail and head south over less intimidating terrain toward increasingly dramatic Navajo.

Two gullies lead up to a low point on the skyline between Niwot Ridge and Navajo Peak. Ascend the gully on the left, which is not blocked by cliffs. This is called "airplane gully" because the wreckage from a January 21, 1948, plane crash litters its length, together with a difficult assemblage of small rocks called scree that constantly slip under boots to carry climbers back downhill. This tiresome stuff also can crash down to hit fellow climbers. Stay close to climbing companions, catch whatever dislodged rocks you can, and shout warnings when a falling stone demands that climbers lift their eyes to dodge what is coming.

It is a trial, but I do not believe anyone has died here since three Civil Aeronautics Administration staff were caught in a down draft that crashed their C-47's flight from Denver to Grand Junction. Searchers needed four months to locate the crash site, from which the bodies eventually were recovered.

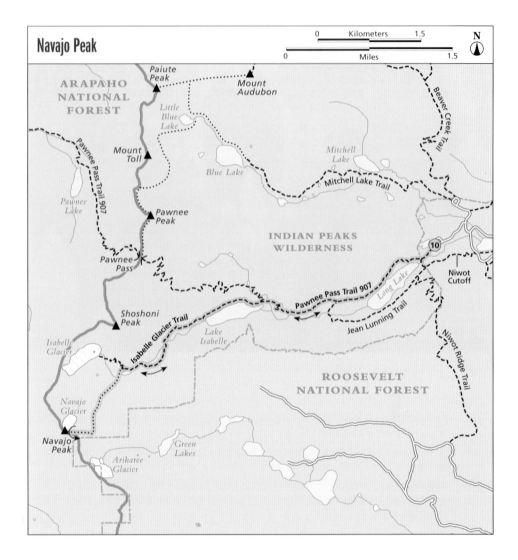

Navajo Peak

0   Kilometers   1.5
0   Miles   1.5

N

Paiute Peak

ARAPAHO
NATIONAL
FOREST

Mount Audubon

Little Blue Lake

Mount Toll

Blue Lake

Mitchell Lake

Mitchell Lake Trail

Pawnee Lake

Pawnee Pass Trail 907

Pawnee Peak

INDIAN PEAKS
WILDERNESS

Beaver Creek Trail

10

Pawnee Pass

Niwot Cutoff

Shoshoni Peak

Isabelle Glacier Trail

Pawnee Pass Trail 907

Long Lake

Jean Lunning Trail

Isabelle Glacier

Lake Isabelle

ROOSEVELT
NATIONAL FOREST

Niwot Ridge Trail

Navajo Glacier

Navajo Peak

Green Lakes

Arikaree Glacier

At the top of the gully, turn right to ascend the steep southwestern ridge of Navajo toward the band of cliffs that circles the summit. A vertical gully or chimney at the base of the southeastern section of the tower provides a route-finding climb that is not technically difficult to the top. Gaiters that would have been handy to keep the rocks out of boots on the way up will be even more appreciated on the way down.

Miles and Directions

0.0   Leave Long Lake Trailhead.

0.2   Arrive at Long Lake and the east junction with the Jean Lunning Trail. Keep right to follow Pawnee Pass Trail along the north shore of Long Lake.

This Navajo necklace and blanket typify art for which the tribe is famous.

1.2	Hike past the east end of Jean Lunning Trail where it rejoins the Pawnee Pass Trail from the south shore of Long Lake.
2.1	Arrive at Lake Isabelle where Pawnee Pass Trail climbs to the right. Continue left over a low ridge to Lake Isabelle and follow the path along the north shore.
3.6	Leave Isabelle Glacier Trail at "Isabelle Tarn" and bear by least steep route for "airplane gully." This gully is below the left low point of two low points on the ridge between Niwot Ridge and Navajo Peak.
4.3	Escape from "airplane gully" to follow a here-and-there climbers' trace to the band of cliffs around the summit.
5.0	Exit a chimney to the summit of Navajo.
10.0	Arrive back at the Long Lake Trailhead.

11 Pawnee Pass

Pawnee Pass Trail follows a well-thought-out route offering spectacular views of Navajo Peak and Lake Isabelle (when it is present).

Start: Long Lake Trailhead
Hiking time: About 7 hours
Distance: 8 miles out and back
Difficulty: Moderate
Trail surface: Dirt with some rocky areas above tree line
Best season: Summer
Other trail users: Hikers only
Canine compatibility: Dogs are permitted on handheld, 6-foot leashes
Fees and permits: A vehicle fee good for 3 days provides access to trailheads located in Brainard Lake Recreation Area. Camping is prohibited

Trail contacts: USDA Forest Service, Boulder Ranger District, 3140 Yarmouth Ave., Boulder CO 80301; (303) 541-2500; fs.usda .gov/arp
Maps: Trails Illustrated Indian Peaks Gold Hill; USGS Monarch Lake, Ward
Highlights: subalpine forest, Long Lake, wildflowers, Lake Isabelle, alpine tundra
Wildlife: Mule deer, red squirrel, gray jay, mountain chickadee, moose
Long Lake Trailhead elevation: 10,480 feet
Pawnee Pass elevation: 12,541 feet

Finding the trailhead: To reach trailheads in the Brainard Lake Recreation Area, drive to the historic mining town of Ward on Colorado Hwy. 72. Just north of Ward, turn west on paved Brainard Lake Road to Brainard Lake Recreation Area. A fee collection booth is 2.7 miles up the road. Less than a half mile further is Red Rock Lake on the left side of the road. The lake presents a good view of Indian Peaks and water lilies covering the lake's surface. You will not see water lilies further on. You might see moose feeding in the lake, a sight often seen by hikers on the trails ahead. Brainard Lake is 1.7 miles beyond Red Rock Lake. Proceed around the lake's end. Take the road left to Long Lake Trailhead and the Pawnee Pass Trail. **GPS:** N40° 04' .674"/W105° 35' .007"

The Hike

Pawnee Pass received its name by passing Pawnee Peak, named as part of the process of naming Indian Peaks. The Pawnee were an agricultural people, living in dome-shaped earth lodges in Kansas and Nebraska. They ventured into Colorado's eastern plains to hunt bison while the corn and squash were maturing. It is likely that they did not have much cause to cross the present Pawnee Pass. However, other Native Americans did follow a similar trail across the next low point to the south. This was the Breadline Trail.

For reasons unclear, the Union Pacific Railroad recruited Indians in Canada to act as porters carrying food, including bread, to surveyors figuring out a route for tracks across the mountains in 1882. The surveyors laid out a rail route up the South Saint Vrain Creek valley, which they would fill with rock blasted from a tunnel through the Continental Divide above Lake Isabelle. This engineering marvel would include high

Pawnee Lake sits below Pawnee Pass below spires on the west side of Pawnee Peak.

trestles that would lift the trains in a giant double loop above their own tracks at the gentle grade required by railroads.

It seems not to be mere historic hindsight to wonder why anyone thought this spiritual nightmare might have been other than an analogous economic disaster. One person with moderately clear eyesight and cheese and crackers in a pack could have spent a day wandering up the South Saint Vrain to see that this notion was clearly crazy. Instead, the UP sent out a team of engineers backed up by Native American porters to prove the historic truth that some knowledge is indeed useless. It is easy to imagine some Union Pacific executive back in Omaha reading the survey report, shrugging, and thinking, "Well, that didn't work."

Confirming the existence of good fortune or divine intervention, a path rather than a railroad branches uphill (right) just east of Lake Isabelle. From the lake level, the Pawnee Pass Trail climbs for a bit before bending left (west) along a contour above Lake Isabelle. Through a series of switchbacks, the trail eventually reaches a good lookout of the lake and Navajo Peak from approximately 1,000 feet above the lake. Thrilling views continue as the path winds through yet more switchbacks, leaving vivid tundra flowers behind as it passes into boulders, then reaches more tundra gardens at Pawnee Pass.

West of the pass, the trail descends to Pawnee Lake through superb construction of a sinuous trail framed by spires on the west side of Pawnee Peak. The trail continues eventually to Monarch Lake, described in the account of the Pawnee Lake hike (Hike 41).

Rydbergia are the largest of alpine tundra plants, here blooming above Pawnee Pass on Pawnee Peak.

Pawnee Pass

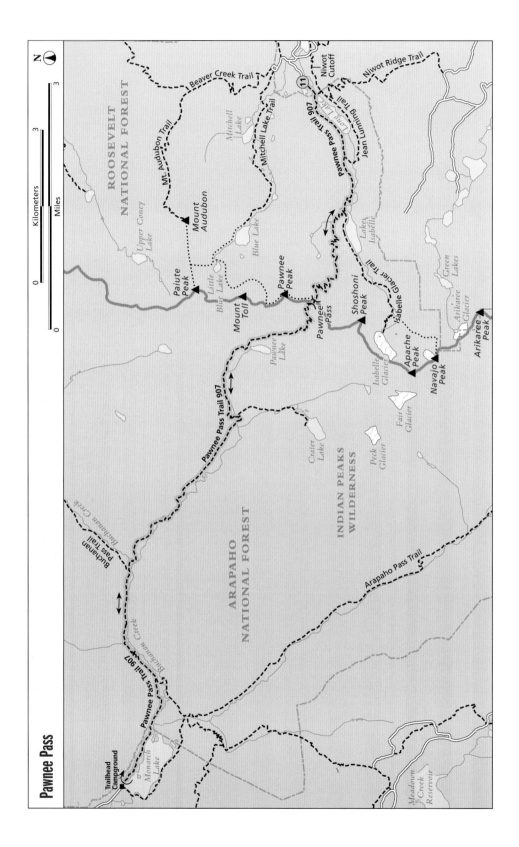

N

Kilometers
0   3   3

Miles
0   3   3

ROOSEVELT NATIONAL FOREST

Beaver Creek Trail

Niwot Cutoff

Niwot Ridge Trail

Mt. Audubon Trail

Upper Coney Lake

Mitchell Lake

Mitchell Lake Trail

907

Pawnee Pass Trail

Jean Lunning Trail

Long Lake

11

Mount Audubon

Paiute Peak

Little Blue Lake

Blue Lake

Pawnee Peak

Mount Toll

Lake Isabelle

Pawnee Pass

Glacier Trail

Shoshoni Peak

Isabelle

Green Lakes

Arikaree Glacier

Pawnee Lake

Isabelle Glacier

Apache Peak

Navajo Peak

Arikaree Peak

Crater Lake

Pawnee Pass Trail 907

Fair Glacier

Peck Glacier

INDIAN PEAKS WILDERNESS

ARAPAHO NATIONAL FOREST

Buchanan Pass Trail

Buchanan Creek

Buchanan Creek

Arapaho Pass Trail

Pawnee Pass Trail 907

Trailhead

Campground

Monarch Lake

Meadow Creek Reservoir

Miles and Directions

0.0   Leave Long Lake Trailhead.

0.2   Arrive at Long Lake and the junction with the Jean Lunning Trail. Continue right on the Pawnee Pass Trail.

1.2   West end of Jean Lunning Trail rejoins Pawnee Pass Trail from south shore of Long Lake.

2.1   Arrive at the trail junction just east of Lake Isabelle, where the Pawnee Pass Trail climbs right for an aerial view of the lake.

2.75   Rise above tree line.

4.5   Arrive at Pawnee Pass.

4.55   Venture west to look down on Pawnee Lake.

9.01   Arrive back at the Long Lake Trailhead.

12 Pawnee Peak

Start: Long Lake Trailhead
Hiking time: About 8 hours
Distance: 10.1 miles out and back
Difficulty: Moderate
Trail surface: Dirt
Best season: Summer
Other trail users: Hikers only
Canine compatibility: Dogs are permitted on 6-foot handheld leash
Fees and permits: A vehicle fee good for 3 days provides access to trailheads located in Brainard Lake Recreation Area. Camping is prohibited except in Pawnee Campground

Trail contacts: USDA Forest Service, Boulder Ranger District, 2140 Yarmouth Ave., Boulder CO 80301; (303) 541-2500; fs.usda .gov/arp
Maps: Trails Illustrated Indian Peaks Gold Hill; USGS Ward, Monarch Lake
Highlights: Long Lake, Lake Isabelle, Pawnee Pass, alpine tundra
Wildlife: Red squirrel, mountain chickadee, moose, mule deer, elk, white-tailed ptarmigan, yellow-belled marmot, pika
Long Lake Trailhead elevation: 10,480 feet
Pawnee Peak elevation: 12,943 feet

Finding the trailhead: To reach trailheads in Brainard Lake Recreation Area, drive to the historic mining town of Ward on Colorado Hwy. 72. Just north of Ward, turn west on paved Brainard Lake Road to Brainard Lake Recreation Area. A fee collection booth is 2.7 miles up the road. Less than a half mile further is Red Rock Lake on the left side of the road. The lake is covered with water lilies (which you will not see further on) and perhaps will have moose sloshing in the lake. However, you likely do not have time to stop, and moose often appear along trails ahead. Brainard Lake is 1.7 miles beyond Red Rock Lake. Proceed around the lake's south shore to a fork in the road beyond the lake's west end. Take the road left to Long Lake Trailhead and the Pawnee Pass Trail. **GPS:** N40° 04' .674"/W105° 35' .077"

The Hike

From Pawnee Pass Trail (see description of Hike 11) to reach the summit of Pawnee Peak requires an uncomplicated trudge in thin air up the Continental Divide from the pass. Hikers who are so tired that they lie down to rest are rewarded by fine views of very rugged peaks framed by tiny tundra flowers glowing with various colors. The blooms provide an honorable reason to refrain from rising.

Miles and Directions

0.0 Leave Long Lake Trailhead.
0.2 Arrive at Long Lake and junction of Jean Lunning Trail. Keep right on the Pawnee Pass Trail.
1.2 West end of Jean Lunning Trail rejoins Pawnee Pass Trail from Long Lake's southern shore.
2.1 Pawnee Pass Trail cuts to the right uphill just east of Lake Isabelle (out of sight behind low ridge).
2.75 Pawnee Pass Trail climbs above tree line.
4.5 Arrive at Pawnee Pass.

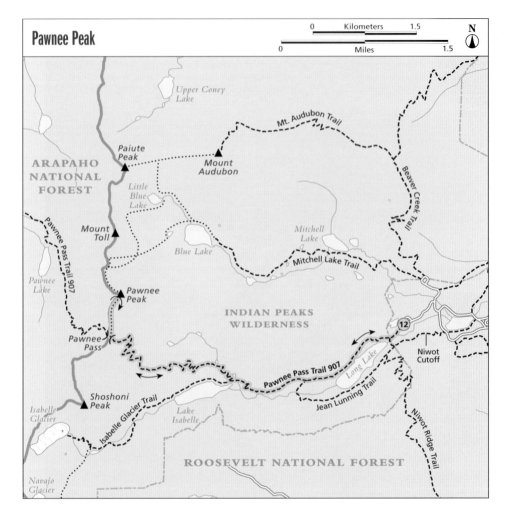

Pawnee Peak

4.55   Venture west along trail to look down at Pawnee Lake framed by rock spires on west flank of Pawnee Peak.

5.05   After simple trudging up a tundra slope, arrive at top of Pawnee.

10.1   Arrive back at the Long Lake Trailhead.

PAWNEE

Normally, the Pawnee farmed corn, beans, and squash in Nebraska and Kansas where they lived in permanent villages of dome-shaped earth lodges. In summer, however, they did leave their maturing crops to hunt (primarily bison) in Colorado, perhaps within sight of Indian Peaks, thus beginning the state's tourism industry in the late eighteenth century.

Horse nomads called Pawnees "wolf people." No wolves currently reside in Indian Peaks.

These agricultural Indians came most dramatically to the attention of the non-Indian farmers in Colorado as allies against horse-nomads who lived in mobile villages of skin tipis. Arapaho, Cheyenne, and Comanche horse-nomads, each in their different languages, called the Pawnees "wolf people." It was not a term of endearment.

For their part, the Pawnee referred to the Cheyenne by their striped arrows, with which the Pawnee were too familiar. They called Arapahos "dog eaters." Pawnee called the Comanche "Larihta," which I do not understand, but the Wichita tribe, linguistically related to the Pawnee, called the Comanche "snakes," which likely captures the meaning.

The Pawnee were favorite targets of horse-nomad raiders because the farmers necessarily lived at known places, near their fields. The bison-dependent horse-nomads, though, were difficult to find for retaliation in the vastness of the Great Plains. Thus, when US Army Major Frank North sought to recruit Pawnee to fight horse-nomads, he got an enthusiastic response. They set out in 1869 to join with regular army troops hunting Cheyenne Dog Soldiers led by Tall Bull.

Tall Bull had been raiding homesteaders and travelers in the vicinity of the present Kansas/Colorado boundary the previous year. Tall Bull was angry at the Euro-Americans because a federal bureaucrat had failed to give him guns and ammunition promised in an 1867 peace treaty. When the Feds had learned that Tall Bull was using these weapons to kill Indian farmers instead of bison, the bureaucrats considered this to be contrary to the treaty terms. They cut off the flow of arms. Tall Bull thought that American objection to his generations-old right to kill Indian farmers and steal their women, stock, and corn was absurd and highly irritating. Therefore, he substituted homesteaders for Pawnees.

Among Tall Bull's 1869 targets had been a colony of recently arrived Swedes intent on farming in Kansas. They could not speak English, but neither could the Cheyenne. Moreover, the Swedes defined the concept of paleface. They were American enough to attack. The Dog Soldiers took two women and four children from the Swedish colony.

In the vicinity of today's Sterling, Colorado, Major North's 150 Pawnee volunteers together with the US Fifth Cavalry found Tall Bull's camp. At the battle's end, Tall Bull was dead, and his Dog Soldiers were dead or scattered. The Cheyenne had killed one Swedish woman and all the Swedish kids, except one who survived after being left for dead. The other Swedish woman ran from a Cheyenne tipi to her rescuers during the battle. The army and perhaps the Pawnee called it the Battle of Summit Springs. A couple of generations later, Denver high school teacher Ellsworth Bethel likely knew of the fight when he placed the name Pawnee on a prominent summit in Indian Peaks.

View from Pawnee Peak summit typifies the ruggedness of Indian Peaks.

13 Mount Toll

Start: Long Lake Trailhead
Hiking time: About 9 hours out and back
Distance: 10 miles circuit
Difficulty: Difficult
Trail surface: Dirt, rock, tundra
Best season: Summer
Other trail users: Hikers only
Canine compatibility: Dogs are permitted on handheld 6-foot leashes
Fees and permits: A vehicle fee good for 3 days provides access to trailheads located in Brainard Lake Recreation Area. Camping prohibited except in Pawnee Campground

Trail contacts: USDA Forest Service, Boulder Ranger District, 2140 Yarmouth Ave., Boulder CO 80301; (303) 541-2500; fs.usda.gov/arp
Maps: Trails Illustrated Indian Peaks Gold Hill; USGS Monarch Lake, Ward
Highlights: Subalpine Forest, Long Lake, Lake Isabelle, Pawnee Pass, Pawnee Peak, Mount Toll
Wildlife: Red Squirrel, mountain chickadee, moose, yellow-bellied marmot, mule deer, elk, white-tailed ptarmigan, pika
Long Lake Trailhead elevation: 10,480 feet
Mount Toll elevation: 12,979 feet

Finding the trailhead: To reach trailheads in the Brainard Lake area, drive to the historic mining town of Ward on Colorado Hwy. 72. Just north of Ward, turn west on paved Brainard Lake Road to Brainard Lake Recreation Area. A fee collection booth is 2.7 miles up the road. Less than a half mile further is Red Rock Lake on the left side of the road. The lake is covered with water lilies; the view of Indian Peaks is great; there might be moose. But you do not have time for any of it. Brainard Lake is 1.7 miles beyond Red Rock Lake. Proceed around Brainard Lake's south shore to a fork in the road beyond the lake's west end. To the left is Long Lake Trailhead, where the hike begins; to the right is Mitchell Creek Trailhead where you will return. The Forest Service has installed a walkway between the two trailheads to keep hikers out of the most dangerous part of the hike, the road. If you arrive at Long Lake Trailhead early enough to make it to the top of Pawnee Peak and then Mount Toll, you likely will be early enough to get a parking spot at the trailhead. **GPS:** N40° 04' .674"/W105° 35' .077"

The Hike

Mount Toll is best known from its attention-grabbing appearance above Blue Lake. However, the easiest route is to first climb Pawnee Peak (see hikes 11 and 12) and continue down the north slope of Pawnee into the broad saddle between Pawnee and Toll. Much of the route-finding up the trackless south slope of Toll is a slog through loose rock (talus). The top is near where the rock eventually gets firm.

The talus is somewhat easier on the descent. Gaiters are useful to keep gravel out of boots. Back in the saddle between Pawnee and Toll, hikers can choose to retrace their steps over Pawnee Peak down to Pawnee Pass Trail, followed by Lake Isabelle and Long Lake. This route permits a variation of adding half a mile to the hike by turning right before reaching Long Lake, to follow the south shore along the Jean Lunning Trail, assuming an ascent in the dawn's early dark along the north shore on the Pawnee Pass Trail.

Mount Toll towers above Little Blue Lake as viewed from Paiute Peak.

14 Mitchell Lake

Mitchell Lake is a transition from deep subalpine forest to open alpine vistas of Mount Toll.

Start: Mitchell Creek Trailhead
Hiking time: About 1.5 hours
Distance: 2.5 miles out and back
Difficulty: Easy
Trail surface: Dirt
Best season: Summer
Other trail users: Hikers only
Canine compatibility: Dogs are permitted on handheld, 6-foot leashes
Fees and permits: A vehicle fee good for 3 days provides access to trailheads located in Brainard Lake Recreation Area. Camping is prohibited except in Pawnee Campground

Trail contacts: USDA Forest Service, Boulder Ranger District, 2140 Yarmouth Ave., Boulder CO 80301; (303) 541-2500; fs.usda. gov/arp
Maps: Trails Illustrated Indian Peaks Gold Hill; USGS Ward
Highlights: Subalpine forest, Mitchell Lake below Mount Toll
Wildlife: Red squirrel, mountain chickadee, and moose
Mitchell Creek Trailhead elevation: 10,480 feet
Mitchell Lake elevation: 10,720 feet

Finding the trailhead: To reach trailheads in the Brainard Lake Recreation Area, drive to the historic mining town of Ward on Colorado Hwy. 72. Just north of Ward, turn west on paved Brainard Lake Road to Brainard Lake Recreation Area. A fee collection booth is 2.7 miles up the road. Less than a half mile further is Red Rock Lake on the left side of the road. It presents a fine view of Indian Peaks, different from that which appears from the Mitchell Creek Trail, as well as water lilies covering the lake's surface. You will not see water lilies further on. However, you may see moose sloshing in Red Rock Lake as well as along the Mitchell Creek drainage. Brainard Lake is 1.7 miles beyond Red Rock Lake. Continue around the south shore of Brainard to a point beyond the lake's west end where the road splits. Take the right branch to Mitchell Lake and Beaver Creek/Mount Audubon trails. Arrive early to find trailhead parking, which will be the most challenging aspect of the hike. **GPS:** N40° 001' .674"/W105° 34' .910"

The Hike

The trail to Mitchell Lake leaves from a trailhead on the left (southwest) side of its parking lot. Understandably, the lot often fills early, and the Forest Service has built a stretch of pathway to reach it on foot from parking areas further east. The trail passes at once into classic, mature, subalpine forest of Engelmann spruce and subalpine fir. The grade is very mild and easy to walk.

Near a bridge where Mitchell Creek briefly muffles the chattering of red squirrels ever objecting to hiker presence is the wilderness boundary. The forest opens to provide a view across the lake of the rock-covered slope of Mount Audubon. But, the

Mount Toll towers above Mitchell Lake.

Hikers to Mitchell Lake are very likely to see unafraid gray jays.

Mitchell Lake

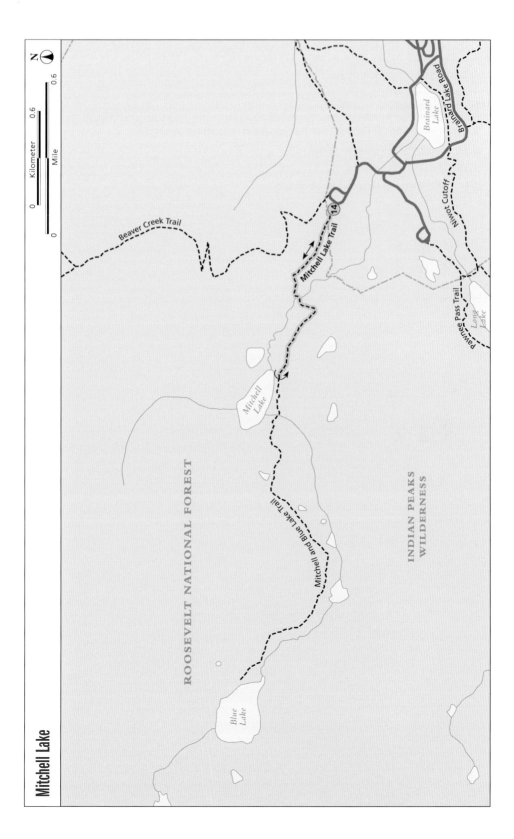

N

Kilometer
0   0.6   0.6

Mile
0   0.6

Beaver Creek Trail

Mitchell Lake Trail

14

Mitchell and Blue Lake Trail

ROOSEVELT NATIONAL FOREST

INDIAN PEAKS
WILDERNESS

Blue
Lake

Mitchell
Lake

Pawnee Pass Trail

Niwot Cutoff

Long
Lake

Brainard
Lake

Brainard Lake Road

best view is had by taking a narrow wooden walkway to the lake's eastern shore for an exciting view of Mount Toll.

Miles and Directions

0.0   Leave on trail to Mitchell Lake from southwest (left) side of parking lot.

0.5   Cross Mitchell Creek on bridge.

1.25   Arrive at Mitchell Lake.

2.5   Arrive back at Mitchell Creek Trailhead.

15 Blue Lake

Blue Lake's name is so mundane that hikers reaching its shore for the first time may be shocked by the lake's drama.

Start: Mitchell Creek Trailhead
Hiking time: About 4 hours
Distance: 5 miles out and back
Difficulty: Easy
Trail surface: Dirt
Best season: Summer
Other trail users: Hikers only
Canine compatibility: Dogs are permitted on handheld, 6-foot leashes
Fees and permits: A vehicle fee good for 3 days provides access to trailheads located in Brainard Lake Recreation Area. Camping is prohibited except in Pawnee Campground

Trail contacts: USDA Forest Service, Boulder Ranger District, 2140 Yarmouth Ave., Boulder CO 80301; (303) 541-2500; fs.usda .gov/arp
Maps: Trails Illustrated Indian Peaks Gold Hill; USGS Ward
Highlights: Mitchell Lake and Blue Lake
Wildlife: Moose, yellow-bellied marmot, red squirrel, and mountain chickadee
Mitchell Creek Trailhead elevation: 10,480 feet
Blue Lake elevation: 11,320 feet

Finding the trailhead: To reach trailheads in the Brainard Lake Recreation Area, drive to the historic mining town of Ward on Colorado Hwy. 72. Just north of Ward, turn west on paved Brainard Lake Road to Brainard Lake Recreation Area. A fee collection booth is 2.7 miles up the road. Less than a half mile further is Red Rock Lake on the left side of the road. The lake presents a good view of Indian Peaks, and water lilies cover the lake's surface. You will not see water lilies further on. You might see moose feeding in the lake, a sight seen often by hikers on the trails ahead. Brainard Lake is 1.7 miles beyond Red Rock Lake. Proceed along the south shore of Brainard Lake to a split in the road beyond the lake's west end. Take the road to the right to the trails to Mitchell Lake and Mount Audubon. The trail to Mitchell and Blue lakes begins on the southwest side of the parking lot. Arrive early, very early, to find a parking spot at the trailhead, or plan to drive back east to find parking which adds to the length of the hike. **GPS:** N40° 05' .001"/W105° 34' .910"

The Hike

Blue Lake is not notably bluer than Blue Lake to the north in Rocky Mountain National Park's Glacier Gorge. The Indian Peaks Blue Lake, because it is relatively close to its trailhead, frequently receives its visitors early enough in the day to catch the reflection from the blue sky, which doubtless encouraged its naming. However, many hikers arrive early enough in the season to see the lake's surface covered by ice and any blue in the water is scarcely noticeable. The introduction to this spectacle also is very impressive. An easy walk through magnificent subalpine forest opens on Mitchell Lake, the first of trailside vistas of Mount Toll.

Parry primrose bloom in Mitchell Creek.

Beyond Mitchell Lake, hikers leave the dense woods for more open and somewhat steeper terrain.

At tree line, a major snowfield across the trail melts throughout the summer, watering one of my favorite displays of Parry primrose. This foot-tall wildflower is in the running for the title of most spectacular subalpine and alpine flower. Its intense magenta blossoms, which seem to glow from within, decorate bogs, stream banks, and other wet areas. Their red hue is due to one of the chemicals known as anthocyanins. The flower's smell is far less pleasant than its color, both of which help attract pollinating insects. Happily, Parry primrose is fairly common, but this is my favorite site to enjoy its color because it is reasonable to suppose that here or nearby is where pioneering botanist Charles Parry likely discovered the type specimen for this plant in 1864.

As is common with glacier-carved tarns, Blue Lake is hidden from below, which adds to its impact when hikers arrive on its shore. Mount Toll rises 1,659 feet from the surface with a waterfall plunging into 25 acres of water at the base of the mountain. Tundra patches on the eastern shore contrast with boulders that surround most of the lake. The glacier-gouged basin containing Blue Lake is presumed to be 100 feet deep, a convenient-to-remember number. But, 100 feet is disconcerting if you should fall in at the far shore loaded with cameras and boots, freezing in water that was snow at sunrise.

I do not think it has happened, yet.

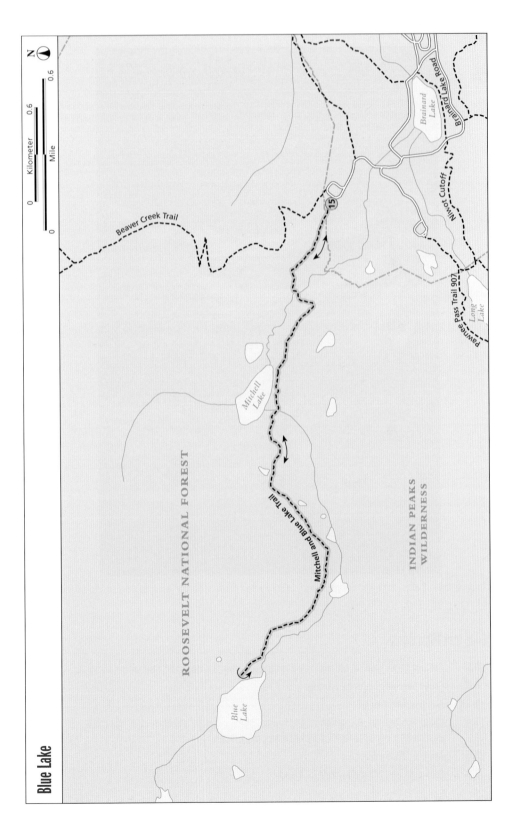

Blue Lake

N

0   0.6   Kilometer
0   0.6   Mile

Beaver Creek Trail

ROOSEVELT NATIONAL FOREST

Mitchell Lake

Blue Lake

Mitchell and Blue Lake Trail

15

INDIAN PEAKS WILDERNESS

Pawnee Pass Trail 907

Long Lake

Niwot Cutoff

Brainard Lake Road

Brainard Lake

Because Blue Lake is close to its trailhead, hikers often reach it in the morning before clouds fill the sky, which thus remains blue to be reflected on the lake's surface.

Miles and Directions

0.0 Set out on the trail to Mitchell Lake on the southwest side of the trailhead parking lot.

0.5 Cross Mitchell Creek on a bridge.

1.25 Arrive at Mitchell Lake.

1.4 Cross Mitchell Creek inlet on a long bridge. Moose can be anywhere, but pay close attention to ponds as the valley becomes more open.

2.5 Arrive at Blue Lake.

5.0 Arrive back at Mitchell Creek Trailhead.

16 Mount Audubon

Mount Audubon is the easiest 13,000-foot peak to climb in Indian Peaks.

Start: Beaver Creek Trailhead
Hiking time: About 6 hours
Distance: 7.5 miles out and back
Difficulty: Moderate
Trail surface: Dirt
Best season: Summer
Other trail users: Hikers only
Canine compatibility: Dogs are permitted on handheld, 6-foot leashes
Fees and permits: A vehicle fee good for 3 days provides access to trailheads located in Brainard Lake Recreation Area. Camping prohibited except in Pawnee Campground

Trail contacts: USDA Forest Service, Boulder Ranger District, 2140 Yarmouth Ave., Boulder CO 80301; (303) 541-2500; fs.usda.gov/arp
Maps: Trails Illustrated Indian Peaks and Gold Hill; USGS Ward
Highlights: alpine tundra, Mount Audubon
Wildlife: white-tailed ptarmigan, mountain chickadee, red squirrel, mule deer
Beaver Creek Trail to Mount Audubon trailhead elevation: 10,480 feet
Mount Audubon elevation: 13,223 feet

Finding the trailhead: To reach trailheads in the Brainard Lake area, drive to the historic mining town of Ward on Colorado Hwy. 72. Just north of Ward, turn west on unpaved Brainard Lake Rd to Brainard Lake Recreation Area. A fee collection booth is 2.7 miles up the road. Less than a half mile further is Red Rock Lake on the left side of the road. The lake presents a good view of Indian Peaks and water lilies covering the lake's surface. You will not see water lilies further on. You might see moose feeding in the lake, a sight often seen by hikers on the trails ahead. Brainard Lake is 1.7 miles beyond Red Rock Lake. Continue around the south shore of Brainard Lake to a split in the road beyond Brainard's western end. The right branch leads to the trailhead for Mount Audubon. On the way up make note of any empty parking spaces at Niwot Picnic Area. If you arrive late, you may need to park further east than the trailhead. Additional parking is available in larger lots east of Brainard Lake. **GPS:** N40° 05' .001"/W105° 34' .910"

The Hike

The Beaver Creek Trail to Mount Audubon begins at the right side of the trailhead parking lot. Ascending northwest through typical subalpine forest for a half mile, the path reaches a long set of switchbacks. At the west end of the second switchback is an excellent view of Mount Toll rising behind a steep, rocky slope of Mount Audubon. Limber pine predominates as the trail zigzags then reverts to scrubby spruce and fir near tree line.

The trail enters Indian Peaks Wilderness 1.7 miles from the trailhead. It splits a short way above tree line, the right fork continuing straight, eventually descending to Coney Flats Trailhead. The Mount Audubon Trail heads west (left), bending up a gradual tundra slope. July to mid-August, displays of alpine wildflowers are very good.

The rugged view southwest from the top of Mount Audubon includes Navajo and Apache peaks.

This trail up a mountain named Audubon (see sidebar) may be the most appropriate place in Colorado to look for birds, even though you may not see more than a half dozen species above the trees. The most sought after of these species is also the toughest to spot. Summer feathers of white-tailed ptarmigan make the birds look so much like the lichen-covered rocks protruding from carpets of tundra plants that the birds are perfectly camouflaged. Evolved not to move, they are fairly common along the trail and are likely to remain unnoticed unless nearly kicked by an unaware hiker's booted foot. When the ptarmigan darts away to avoid the boot, the hiker invariably is startled by a running rock and likely flinches before grinning because of the good luck.

The trail winds across tundra toward a large snowbank, then switchbacks to the right. Terrain is very rocky in the switchbacks, ideal habitat for cushion plants such as moss campion. Eventually, the switchbacks climb to a gentler grade within the saddle immediately north of the main bulk of Audubon. A left turn leads to a steep climb, hopefully following cairns and bits of trail to the top.

On the way, watch for big-rooted spring beauty. Its white blossoms tinged with pink bloom around a large rosette of fleshy leaves, which turn bright red in autumn. This plant seems more common on Audubon and the rest of Indian Peaks than further north in Rocky Mountain National Park.

White-tailed ptarmigan mimics lichen-covered rocks in alpine tundra meadow on the north side of Mount Audubon.

Mount Audubon

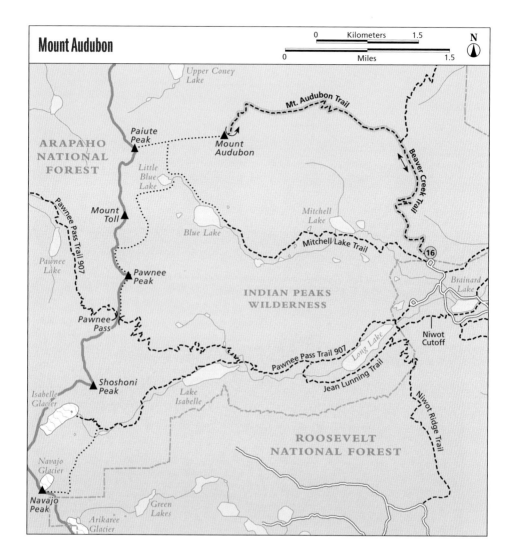

Miles and Directions

0.0 Begin at the Beaver Creek Trailhead to Mount Audubon on the right side of the trailhead parking lot.

0.25 Watch for the trail to bend left, which is easy to miss if snow covers the trail. Handily, Audubon is the first trail to melt out in spring.

1.4 Cross above tree line.

1.7 The Beaver Creek Trail and Mount Audubon Trail split. Head left on the Mount Audubon Trail.

3.5 Reach the saddle north of the main bulk of Mount Audubo.

3.75 Top out on the summit of Mount Audubon.

7.5 Arrive back at Beaver Creek Trailhead.

JOHN JAMES AUDUBON

John James Audubon was a great painter and researcher of North American birds during the first decades of the nineteenth century. His reputation makes him the bird painter to whom all subsequent bird artists are compared. He began as a struggling artist wandering through the deciduous forests of the upper Midwest, searching for birds to portray while his business ventures failed. Infrequently credited in the shadow of her eventually famous husband, his wife, Lucy, was a constant support during these difficult years.

Failing to find backing in America for his efforts to portray American birds, Audubon sailed to England to seek sponsors. His work was an immediate hit. He was hailed as a genius, and honors and success followed for the rest of his life. When he decided that his work with birds (perhaps a thousand paintings) was sufficient, he started to be equally thorough with North American mammals. He traveled on the Missouri River as far as Montana to paint western birds, but never explored in what would become Colorado. Audubon died in 1851. So great were his accomplishments that his admirer, Charles Parry, named Mount Audubon only 13 years later.

A botanist who served America much better collecting plants in Colorado than he would have dying in some Civil War trench, Parry was conducting research from a campsite in company of a zoologist, Dr. J. W. Velie. They climbed "a smooth round peak" despite deep snow still present in June. Parry wrote that at the suggestion of Velie, "we concluded to afix to this well-marked elevation the name of the distinguished naturalist Audubon." So, 50 years before Ellsworth Bethel conceived of naming the peaks north of Arapaho Pass for Native American tribes, Mount Audubon, thanks to pioneering naturalists following Audubon's example, stood conspicuously in the middle of Indian Peaks. The great naturalist clearly merited the honor, and Bethel recommended that the name stick. In contrast, Bethel was extremely irate with the name of extremely prominent Mount Alice, claiming (reasonably) that this spoiled the whole system as no one knew who Alice was.

17 Paiute Peak Circle

Paiute Peak provides a rare and exciting circle trip.

Start: Beaver Creek Trailhead
Hiking time: About 10 hours
Distance: 8.1 miles circuit
Best season: Summer
Other trail users: Hikers only
Canine compatibility: Dogs are permitted with handheld, 6-foot leashes
Fees and permits: A vehicle fee good for 3 days provides access to trailheads located in Brainard Lake Recreation Area. Camping is prohibited except in Pawnee Campground
Trail contacts: USDA Forest Service, Boulder Ranger District, 2140 Yarmouth Ave., Boulder CO 80301; (303) 541-2500; fs.usda.gov/arp

Maps: Trails Illustrated Indian Peaks Gold Hill; USGS Monarch Lake, Ward
Highlights: Subalpine forest, alpine tundra, Mount Audubon, Paiute Peak, Blue Lake, and Mitchell Lake
Wildlife: White-tailed ptarmigan, mountain chickadee, red squirrel, moose
Beaver Creek Trail to Mount Audubon trailhead elevation: 10,480 feet
Mount Audubon elevation: 13,233 feet
Paiute Peak elevation: 13,088 feet

Finding the trailhead: To reach trailheads in the Brainard Lake area, drive to the historic mining town of Ward on Colorado Hwy. 72. Just north of Ward, turn west on paved Brainard Lake Road to Brainard Lake Recreation Area. A fee collection booth is 2.7 miles up the road. Less than a half mile further is Red Rock Lake on the left side of the road. It should be dark when you get there, so drive on by water lilies and potential moose. You might see moose from trails ahead. Brainard Lake is 1.7 miles beyond Red Rock Lake. Continue around the south side of Brainard Lake to a split in the road beyond the lake's western end. Take the right branch to the trailhead for Mitchell Lake and Beaver Creek trails. The Beaver Creek Trail up Mount Audubon begins on the right side of the trailhead parking lot. **GPS:** N40° 05' .001"/W105° 34' .91"

The Hike

The easiest route to Paiute Peak begins at the Beaver Creek Trail up Mount Audubon on the north side of the trailhead parking lot. Switchbacks lessen the effort of following the trail amid subalpine forest into limber pine followed by more subalpine fir and Engelmann spruce reduced to scrubby growth by wind and cold at tree line. Above the trees, a tundra junction leads left up Audubon (see Hike 16). From a broad saddle on the north flank of Mount Audubon, the way follows cairns and scraps of path steeply over boulders to the top of Audubon.

To continue to Paiute Peak, descend a southwestern ridge on the other side of Audubon from the ascent route. From the saddle between Audubon and Paiute, the easiest route tends toward the northern side of the ridge, leading to Paiute's summit. Take care; high cliffs drop steeply on all sides. Paiute has claimed the lives of two climbers in separate incidents.

View southwest from Paiute Peak looks into drainage of Thunderbolt Creek.

To take advantage of the rare pleasures of a circle route, descend from the low point in the ridge between Paiute Peak and Mount Audubon. A very steep gully leads to informally named "Little Blue Lake." There is much loose rock in this gully. Slight knowledge of physics reveals that all this rock did not originate from below. Watch carefully for falling rock and step lightly to avoid kicking more onto any other climbers. Also, beware of hazardous snowfields with steepness that can lead to an uncontrolled, fatal slide into rocks.

When you finally reach Blue Lake, a faint route follows the north edge of the lake. Most likely, weariness and resultant clumsiness will have set in; a fall into water that was ice the day before while you are burdened with boots and a gear-filled pack would create serious problems for a team trying to recover your body from the presumed 100-foot depth of the lake.

From the east end of Blue Lake, an easy trail winds 2.5 miles back to the trailhead parking lot. Because this exciting circle trip requires an early start, you likely were able to find a parking spot at the trailhead to take advantage of one of the very few circuits that does not require shuffling of cars.

Blue Lake (at the top) and Little Blue Lake invite climbers descending from Paiute Peak.

Miles and Directions

0.0   Leave the trailhead on Beaver Creek Trail to Mount Audubon from the right side of the parking lot.

0.25   The trail bends left, a turn easy to miss when covered by snow. Mount Audubon usually is the first destination to melt out in spring.

1.4   Climb above tree line.

1.7   Mount Audubon Trail heads left from Beaver Creek Trail. Climb left.

2.5	Enter the saddle north of the mass of Mount Audubon for a good view of Longs Peak and Mount Meeker to the north in Rocky Mountain National Park.
3.75	Reach the top of Mount Audubon.
4.52	Carefully teeter on the low point of the ridge between Mount Audubon and Paiute Peak.
4.75	Arrive at the top of Paiute Peak.
4.97	Return to the low point of the ridge between Mount Audubon and Paiute Peak.
5.19	Reach base of gully descending from low point of the ridge between Mount Audubon and Paiute Peak.
5.79	Arrive at Little Blue Lake.
6.01	Arrive at Blue Lake's eastern end.
7.26	Celebrate arrival at Mitchell Lake's eastern end with views of Mount Toll.
8.1	Arrive back at the south end of the trailhead parking lot.

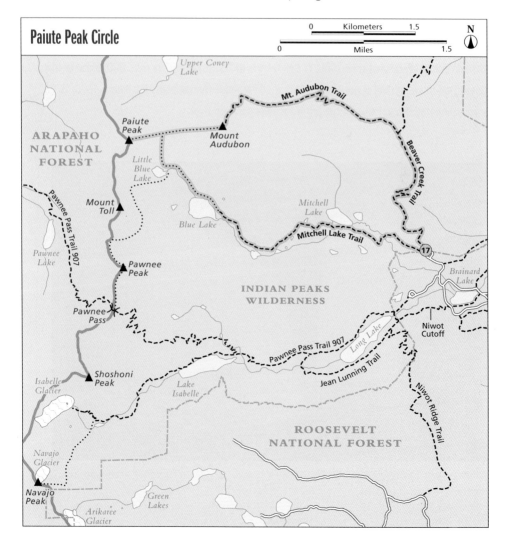

COMPROMISE

Compromise rarely pleases anyone. A century ago, Paiute was a compromise for those advocating the obviously appropriate plan of using Indian names on the line of spectacular mountains forming the western skyline of Front Range communities. Indian Peaks, they reasoned, should include a Ute Peak because the Utes were such a prominent tribe in the history of the Colorado Rockies.

But for the US Board on Geographic Names, the bureaucracy with the final say about names on the map, Ute prominence was precisely the problem. There already was a confusing collection of Ute names in Colorado. Names were supposed to reduce confusion, not increase it. History had stuck the Board with problems like Cony Lake and Cony Creek being in the valley next to the valley containing Coney Lake and Coney Creek. They were not going to make an inherited problem worse by permitting Ute as a new name for any other place.

The namers had to compromise with Paiute, at that time more of a linguistic group rather than an actual structured tribe living in the deserts of California and Nevada. Both sides of this naming controversy had a good point, hence compromise. Fortunately, for hikers, there is no mountaineering compromise in the joy of ascending Paiute Peak.

Paiute baskets in Eagle Plume collection along Colorado Highway 7 north of Allenspark were used to gather seeds for food.

18 Rainbow Lakes

Observation of Rainbow Lakes demonstrates that lakes are ephemeral features of the landscape.

Start: Entrance to Rainbow Lakes Campground, although campers can intercept the trail from an old route from the western end of the campground
Hiking time: About 3 hours
Distance: 2.6 miles out and back
Difficulty: Easy
Trail surface: Dirt
Best season: Summer
Other trail users: Hikers only
Canine compatibility: Dogs are permitted on handheld, 6-foot leashes
Fees and permits: None for hiking. Permit is required for overnight camping in Rainbow

Lakes Campground and within the Indian Peaks Wilderness Area
Trail contacts: USDA Forest Service, Boulder Ranger District, 2140 Yarmouth Ave., Boulder CO 80301; (303) 541-2500; fs.usda.gov/arp
Maps: Trails Illustrated Indian Peaks Gold Hill; USGS Ward
Highlights: Rainbow Lakes
Wildlife: Moose, mule deer, mountain chickadee, red squirrel, and black bear
Rainbow Lake Trailhead elevation: 10,200 feet
Rainbow Lake # 4 elevation: 10,285 feet

Finding the trailhead: The Rainbow Lakes Trailhead is located east of the entrance to Rainbow Lakes Campground. To reach the campground, drive on Colorado Hwy. 72 for 5 miles south of Ward or 8 miles north of Nederland. Turn west on an unpaved county road identified as the road to the University of Colorado Mountain Research Station. The road forks after 0.8 mile; take the left branch for a 4-mile bumpy drive up to the campground. The new trailhead is located at the campground entrance. **GPS:** N40° 1' .18"/W105° 36' .52"

The Hike

From the trailhead at the entrance to Rainbow Lake Campground, it is a half-mile hike to the nearest lake. The trail passes through limber pine/Douglas fir forest above campsites that each comes equipped, significantly, with its own bear-proof locker. A sign at the campground entrance warns against hanging hummingbird feeders, which seemingly do double duty, attracting bears as well as hummers. The hummingbirds that otherwise would entertain campers would include broad-tailed hummingbirds joined in August by rufous hummingbirds headed south after mating in Canada. Hikers almost certainly will hear the whine of air passing through slots in the wings of male broadtails. Hikers might see as well as hear these tiny helicopter marvels.

But the hummers are far more hazardous than the bears because the birds divert hikers' eyes from rocks in the trail. These become obviously more prevalent when the

Rainbow Lakes demonstrate plant succession below the alpine tundra.

Lockers in Rainbow Lake Campground encourage harmony between black bears and campers.

Greenback cutthroat trout are rebuilding their population in Rainbow Lakes.

trail crosses the wilderness boundary where the Arapaho Glacier Trial cuts right to climb onto tundra slopes above the trees. More than normal care is needed on a trail left to Rainbow Lakes that is not notably steep but which can send tripping hikers into a bruising or bone-breaking fall.

Typically, the trail bypasses the lakes, and a web of branch paths leads down to the rocky shores. The lakeside views are more often charming than spectacular. Perhaps someone a century ago saw a rainbow at these lakes, but this meteorological phenomenon is no more likely here than elsewhere. Rainbow trout swim in the waters, but in small numbers due to competition from introduced brook trout. Introducing alien brookies, a favored species of anglers, seemed like a good idea until they nearly drove native greenback cutthroat trout into extinction. A reversal in policy removed brookies just in time to support greenbacks enough to alleviate their endangered status. Now, elimination of brook trout to protect greenbacks is a goal that decrees no limits of either number or size on brookie fishing, although it still brings much joy to anglers.

Rainbow Lakes do not mimic the arc of rainbows in their placement relative to each other. Rather they spread in a relatively straight line down a drainage determined millennia ago by a glacier. During a much colder time some 10,000 years ago, a conveyor belt of ice flowing from above either scraped out lake basins or laid down dams of rock to form Rainbow Lakes when the ice melted. Today, as the stream

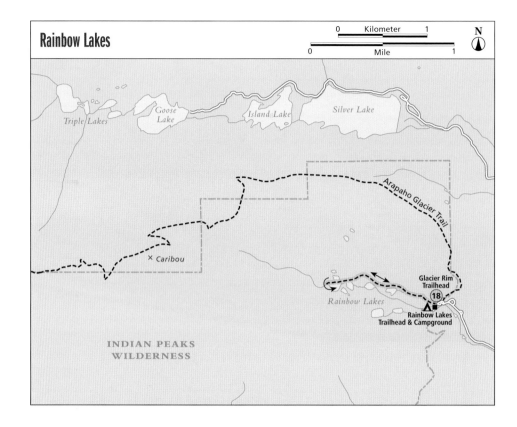

Triple Lakes

Goose
Lake

Island Lake

Silver Lake

Arapaho Glacier Trail

× Caribou

Glacier Rim
Trailhead

18

Rainbow Lakes

Rainbow Lakes
Trailhead & Campground

INDIAN PEAKS
WILDERNESS

which strings together this shining necklace carries silt to fill in the lakes, they present a particularly clear textbook example of plant succession.

Flowing water, when slowed by glacial depression or glacial moraine dams, no longer has the energy to carry its previous load of silt. The silt is dropped where the water slows first, around the lake edges. As the lake fills, it is replaced by successively drier rings of land. The first area to dry, furthest from the lake's center, eventually provides soil for native forest of short-needled conifers and other plants adapted to dry soil. The next and wetter ring toward the center provides home to deciduous willows, food for moose, whose feces hikers almost certainly will see on the trail while watching to avoid tripping on rocks. The next ring of more recent filling are grasses and sedges adapted to yet damper dirt. Then hikers will notice the next interior ring of rock and mud waiting for plant colonization, led by algae, mosses, and liverworts. Next is shallow water, where the lake's bottom is clearly visible. And in the center is open water which may reflect surrounding high mountains (perhaps exceeding 12,000 feet above sea level), tundra-covered but not dramatically carved like the Continental Divide in Indian Peaks.

Some stretches of trail pass willow flats, where once open water had naturally filled in to create willow thickets for moose food and shelter. These were once lakes and will continue to dry until the willows are gone and replaced by a climax forest of conifers and red squirrels, which mark the end of plant succession, until the next glacier comes grinding down. Just how far a lake needs to progress toward this end before it no longer should be called a lake is the cause of some difference of opinion about how many lakes comprise Rainbow Lakes. Some folks count nine, others ten.

Miles and Directions

0.0   Begin at a trailhead recently constructed at entrance to Rainbow Lakes Campground.
0.2   Enter Indian Peaks Wilderness.
1.3   Trail ends at the furthest lake, fourth easily seen from the main trail.
2.6   Arrive back at the trailhead at Rainbow Lakes Campground entrance.

19 Arapaho Glacier

Arapaho Glacier is the most southerly glacier in the Rocky Mountains.

Start: Rainbow Lakes Campground
Hiking time: About 10 hours
Distance: 12 miles in and out
Difficulty: Moderate
Trail surface: Dirt
Best season: Summer
Other trail users: Hikers only
Canine compatibility: Dogs are permitted on handheld, 6-foot leashes
Fees and permits: None for hiking. Permits are required for overnight camping in Rainbow Lakes Campground and in Indian Peaks Wilderness

Trail contacts: USDA Forest Service, Boulder Ranger District, 2140 Yarmouth Ave., Boulder CO 80301; (303) 541-2500; fs.usda.gov/arp
Maps: Trails Illustrated Indian Peaks Gold Hill; USGS Monarch Lake, Ward
Highlights: Alpine tundra, Arapaho Glacier overlook
Wildlife: Moose, mule deer, elk, red squirrel, white-tailed ptarmigan, yellow-bellied marmot, pika, mountain chickadee
Rainbow Lakes Trailhead elevation: 9,960 feet
Arapaho Glacier overlook elevation: 12,710 feet

Finding the trailhead: The Arapaho Glacier Trailhead begins at the entrance to Rainbow Lakes Campground. To reach the campground, drive on Colorado Hwy. 72 for 5 miles south of Ward or 8 miles north of Nederland. Turn west on unpaved CR 116, identified as the road to the University of Colorado Mountain Research Station. The road forks after 0.8 mile. Take the left fork on a bumpy (passable in a normal passenger car) 4-mile drive to the campground. The trailhead is on the right side of the road. **GPS:** N40° 1' .18"/W105° 36' .52"

The Hike

When rufous hummingbirds fly south from Canadian nesting grounds to visit Colorado in August, they cross the world's longest undefended border. Then they reach the border of the Boulder Watershed, which is not undefended.

Competition for water is likely Colorado's largest and perhaps eternal controversy. In 1928, Congress gave to the city of Boulder the land between Niwot Ridge and the drainage below South Arapaho Peak to supply municipal water. Countless signs inform hikers that they must stay out of most of this land of spectacular lakes and peaks. Presumably, the moose, elk, mule deer, cougars, bobcats, weasels, red squirrels, black bears, chipmunks, deer mice, red-backed voles, and hummingbirds also read these signs and refrain from pooping in the pools of the Boulder Watershed, which today provide 40 percent of Boulder's water.

The most significant exception to this ban on mountaineering trespass is the Arapaho Glacier Trail, which climbs to unsurpassed alpine tundra views, coincidentally wanders back and forth between watershed and Indian Peaks Wilderness, and from which hikers constantly are reminded not to stray. From the campground,

Alpine tundra rises above Boulder Watershed below the Continental Divide.

the trail climbs through Douglas-fir and limber pine forest before splitting; left to Rainbow Lakes, right to Arapaho Glacier overlook. Through grades of varying steepness, the Arapaho Glacier Trail follows the watershed boundary for about a mile before heading left and zigzagging nearly to tree line.

From a ridge crest above tree line, hikers can look down at the gorgeous valley of North Boulder Creek. The edge of the watershed is marked, and natural lakes and reservoirs store water below a line of rugged 13,000-foot peaks that form the western horizon along the Continental Divide. North Arapaho to the left and Arikaree on the right are high points in the view. Arikaree was named for a tribe of farmers along the upper Missouri River, but the name in Boulderese translates as "You are forbidden to climb this mountain." Mount Albion is massive across the gorge from the trail, but contrary to its name, is no whiter than other peaks in sight. Therefore, its present translation is identical to Arikaree.

Photographers should compose their pictures of this magnificent scene before following the trail in a sharp left turn up the ridge. Beyond this switchback, the lake-filled valley drops from sight. The peaks still are scenic but appear to rise less dramatically from the tundra slope.

Particularly in July, wildflower jewels carpet that slope up to the narrow trail's edge. Wide switchbacks bend up the slope past moss campion, alpine sunflowers, alpine wallflowers, and dozens of other colorful species. The trail flattens on top of the ridge and passes to the south-facing slope. Above 12,600 feet, the trail undulates for a few miles across unexcelled tundra where alpine flowers compete for attention with hanging lakes

Tundra wildflowers border the Arapaho Glacier Trail.

to the south below rugged peaks. More than 6 miles from Rainbow Lake Campground, the trail joins another rising from the valley of North Fork Middle Boulder Creek.

From the junction, walk uphill a few yards to an overlook of Arapaho Glacier, the most southerly glacier in the Rocky Mountains. Its existence so far south is something of a geographical wonder because glaciers are defined as accumulating enough snow and ice to flow away from the accumulation point for that frozen water, which southern location in North America does not encourage.

If you have arranged for transportation at Fourth of July Trailhead, you can hike down to the remains of the Fourth of July Mine and on out to Fourth of July Trailhead, making it a one-way trip. Or you can relive the wonder and hike back to Rainbow Lakes Campground.

Miles and Directions

0.0   Begin at entrance to Rainbow Lakes Campground.

0.2   Enter Indian Peaks Wilderness.

2.0   Climb above tree line.

6.25 Arrive at overlook of Arapaho Glacier.

12.5 Arrive back at the Rainbow Lakes Campground. Or alternatively, (7.0 miles) descend to remains of Fourth of July Mine (9.0 miles) Meet greenhouse-gas-causing transport at Buckingham Trailhead at Fourth of July Campground (trailhead directions at Hike 20).

Arapaho Glacier

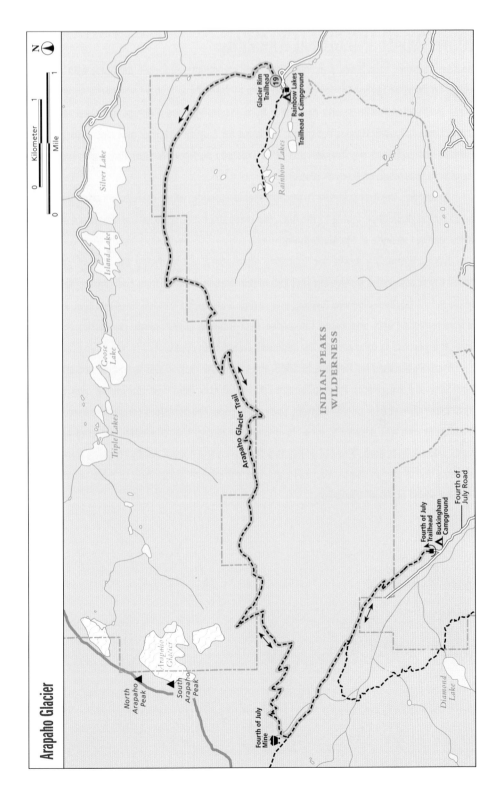

North Arapaho Peak

South Arapaho Peak

Arapaho Glacier

Fourth of July Mine

Silver Lake

Island Lake

Goose Lake

Triple Lakes

Glacier Rim Trailhead

Rainbow Lakes Trailhead & Campground

Rainbow Lakes

Arapaho Glacier Trail

INDIAN PEAKS WILDERNESS

Fourth of July Trailhead

Buckingham Campground

Fourth of July Road

Diamond Lake

19

N

Kilometer

Mile

0   1

0   1

JOHN TYNDALL AND GLOBAL WARMING

Boulder boosters sometimes point out that their community quenches its thirst with glacier water. So do other towns. For instance, the town of Estes Park, a short way north, supplies its water purification facilities with meltwater from several glaciers. Perhaps the most interesting of these is Tyndall Glacier because it is named for English physicist and mountaineer John Tyndall, who explained why Arapaho and other Colorado glaciers are shrinking and losing their movement that qualifies them as glaciers.

Tyndall was the first scientist to quantify global warming, which came to his attention when he observed glaciers shrinking in the Alps. (He made the first ascent of the Weisshorn and one of the earliest ascents of the Matterhorn.)

Tyndall invented a device for capturing atmosphere and analyzing the various gases of which it was composed. He thereby recognized that carbon expelled from coal-burning factories of the industrial revolution was forming into carbon dioxide that trapped the sun's heat, keeping it from reflecting back into space. This added, heat-trapping carbon raised the earth's temperature—this process is what we call the infamous greenhouse effect.

Tyndall published his findings in 1859, the same year that oil was extracted commercially from fields in Pennsylvania. Prior to Thomas Edison's electric light bulb, this oil was used primarily to make kerosene for unsafe lighting. Then along came the horseless carriage powered by oil. Gasoline in cars was deemed to be a clean source of energy that eliminated the need to travel roads ankle deep in horse feces in which flies bred to carry a host of deadly diseases. Now global warming due to carbon combustion melts glaciers and enables mosquitoes to breed more widely to carry a host of deadly diseases.

20 Diamond Lake

You have to squint to see a diamond shape in this lake, but the area around the lake presents the most spectacular wildflower display I ever have seen.

Start: Fourth of July Trailhead above Buckingham Campground

Hiking time: About 4 hours

Distance: 5.4 miles out and back

Difficulty: Moderate

Trail surface: Dirt

Best season: Summer

Other trail users: Hikers only after turn off to Diamond Lake; equestrians on Arapaho Pass Trail (very narrow and steep slope above and below the trail)

Canine compatibility: Dogs are permitted on handheld, 6-foot leashes

Fees and permits: None for hiking or for camping in Buckingham Campground. Permit is required for camping within Indian Peaks Wilderness

Trail contacts: USDA Forest Service, Boulder Ranger District, 2140 Yarmouth Ave., Boulder CO 80301; (303) 541-2500; fs.usda. gov/arp

Maps: Trails Illustrated Indian Peaks Gold Hill; USGS Monarch Lake, Nederland

Highlights: Wildflowers, Diamond Lake

Wildlife: Mule deer, elk, red squirrel, mountain chickadee, chipmunk

Fourth of July Trailhead elevation: 10, 121 feet

Diamond Lake elevation: 10,920 feet

Finding the trailhead: Fourth of July Trailhead at Buckingham Campground is at the end of possibly the worst road that normal passenger cars can travel. A normal car can manage it, just barely, and, in extreme contrast to the trails ahead, it is no fun. To reach this trial begin at Nederland, west of Boulder at the junction of Colorado Hwy. 72 and 119. From the south side of Nederland, a half mile from the joining of these highways, turn west on CR 130 toward the Lake Eldora Ski Area. Where the road forks uphill (left) toward the ski area, continue on the lower (right) fork through the community of Eldora. Its pavement ends shortly. A mile past Eldora, the road forks again. The left fork leads to the Hessie Trailhead (high clearance vehicle recommended). The right fork climbs for rough 4 miles to a parking area at the upper end of the Buckingham Campground and the Fourth of July Trailhead. **GPS:** N39° 59' .714"/W105° 38' .052"

The Hike

Indian Peaks Wilderness and its surroundings produced an incredible amount of mining wealth but no diamond mines. Therefore, perhaps someone in the late nineteenth century thought Diamond Lake was diamond-shaped. Its shape seems more like a teardrop, but its wealth of floral beauty can be compared reasonably to gems.

From the Fourth of July Trailhead above Buckingham Campground, the Arapaho Pass Trail clings to the south flank of South Arapaho Peak. The Buckingham name likely comes from Charles Buckingham, a Boulder banker who enjoyed backcountry experiences exploring Indian Peaks. He also sent surveyors across the wilderness to

North Fork Middle Boulder Creek tumbles through a wild garden along the trail to Diamond Lake.

find a route for a railroad over the Continental Divide in Indian Peaks. Perhaps the best he could do was a trail to Arapaho Pass.

The Diamond Lake Trail drops left from the Arapaho Pass Trail 1.2 miles from Fourth of July Trailhead to cross the North Fork of Middle Boulder Creek. From the particularly lovely creek crossing, the trail twists through subalpine forest for a mile to Diamond Lake. Open meadows present a blooming base to accent views of South Arapaho Peak. Beyond Diamond Lake, the trail passes through subalpine meadows and over a tundra ridge that displays some of the most spectacular flowers in mountains where remarkable flower color is normal. Then it descends to trails leading from the site of the mining town of Hessie.

Assuming your car can still be driven after the road to Buckingham Campground, you may need to return on the same trail you walked to Diamond Lake. However, just to see the flowers, especially around the end of July or first of August, you should push on for at least a mile south of Diamond Lake before returning to Fourth of July Trailhead.

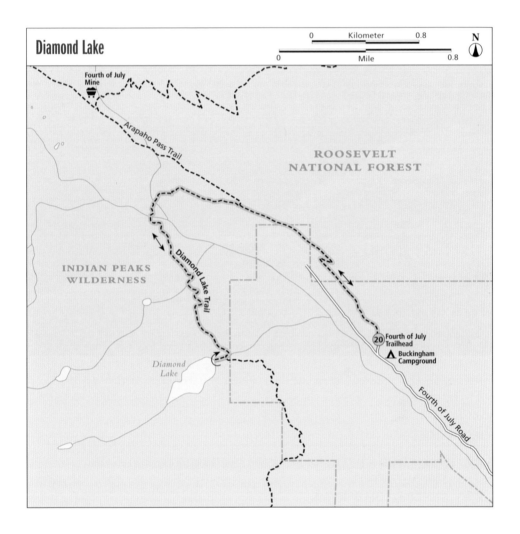

Diamond Lake

0   Kilometer   0.8

0   Mile   0.8

N

Fourth of July
Mine

Arapaho Pass Trail

ROOSEVELT
NATIONAL FOREST

INDIAN PEAKS
WILDERNESS

Diamond Lake Trail

Diamond
Lake

20 Fourth of July
Trailhead

Buckingham
Campground

Fourth of July Road

South Arapaho Peak rises above the best wildflower display in Indian Peaks along the Diamond Lake Trail.

Miles and Directions

0.0   Begin at Fourth of July Trailhead (named for a mine further up the valley) above Buck-ingham Campground.

0.4   Enter Indian Peaks Wilderness.

1.2   From the Arapaho Pass Trail, drop left on the Diamond Lake Trail.

1.7   Cross North Fork of Middle Boulder Creek.

2. 7   Arrive at Diamond Lake.

4.1   If you choose to continue on the Diamond Lake Trail to see the flowers and other beau-ties, it ends at the Devils Thumb Trail.

5.4   Arrive back at the trailhead for what is left of your car.

21 Fourth of July Mine

Although presumably played out now, beginning on Independence Day, 1872, this site marked by rusting mining equipment produced lots of silver.

Start: Buckingham Trailhead at Fourth of July Campground
Hiking time: About 3 hours
Distance: 4 miles out and back
Difficulty: Moderate
Trail surface: Dirt
Best season: Summer
Other trail users: Equestrians
Canine compatibility: Dogs are permitted on handheld, 6-foot leashes
Fees and permits: None for hiking or camping at Buckingham Campground. Permit is required for camping in Indian Peaks Wilderness

Trail contacts: USDA Forest Service, Boulder Ranger District, 2140 Yarmouth Ave., Boulder CO 80310; (303) 541-2500; fs.usda.gov/arp
Maps: Trails Illustrated Indian Peaks Gold Hill; USGS Monarch Lake, Nederland
Highlights: Physical remains of mining history
Wildlife: Red squirrel, mule deer, gray jay, mountain chickadee
Fourth of July Trailhead elevation: 10,121 feet
Fourth of July Mine site elevation: 11,240 feet

Finding the trailhead: Begin at the junction of Colorado Hwy. 72 and 119 in Nederland. From the south side of Nederland, a half mile from the joining of these highways, turn west on CR 132 toward the Lake Eldora Ski Area. Where the road forks uphill (left) toward the ski area, stay on the lower (right) fork through the community of Eldora. Its pavement ends shortly. A mile past Eldora, the road forks again. The left fork leads to the Hessie Trailhead (high clearance vehicle recommended). The right fork climbs for a rough 4 miles to a parking area at the upper end of Fourth of July Campground, near the Buckingham Trailhead. **GPS:** N39° 59' .714"/W105° 38' .052"

The Hike

On Independence Day, 1872, prospector C. C. Alvord proved the virtue of working on holidays when he discovered silver deposits on the south side of South Arapaho Peak. The resulting excavation he called Fourth of July Mine. Today rusting mine remnants still mark the site.

Some hikers maintain that the name identifies the date when snow finally melts enough to open dry-shod access to Arapaho Pass while watering impressive trailside displays of subalpine flowers and ground-hugging tundra flowers. The Arapaho Pass Trail climbs from the Fourth of July Trailhead in a narrow track of consistent grade, clinging to the very steep north wall of the valley of North Fork Middle Boulder Creek. Views across the valley to Mount Neva are impressive. Neva was an Arapaho, whose name Indian Peak namers used to extend the tribe's nomenclature further south from South Arapaho Peak. The trail levels at the mine site before climbing a steep slope to the pass.

Rusty silver mine debris marks the site of the Fourth of July Mine.

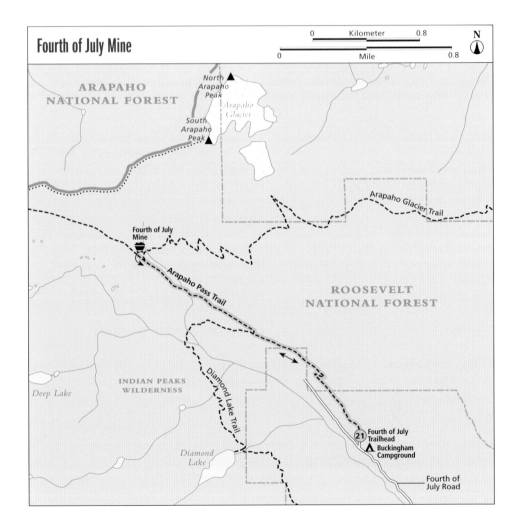

Fourth of July Mine

ARAPAHO NATIONAL FOREST

North Arapaho Peak

Arapaho Glacier

South Arapaho Peak

Fourth of July Mine

Arapaho Glacier Trail

Arapaho Pass Trail

ROOSEVELT NATIONAL FOREST

Diamond Lake Trail

INDIAN PEAKS WILDERNESS

Deep Lake

Diamond Lake

21 Fourth of July Trailhead

Buckingham Campground

Fourth of July Road

Miles and Directions

0.0   Begin on the Arapaho Pass Trail at the Fourth of July Trailhead above Buckingham Campground.

0.4   Enter Indian Peaks Wilderness.

1.2   Diamond Lake Trail drops left to North Fork Middle Boulder Creek.

2.0   Trail levels amid the rusting remnants of mining equipment.

4.0   Arrive back at the Buckingham Trailhead at the Fourth of July Campground.

22 Arapaho Pass

Archeological speculation suggests Native American use of this pass for some 4,000 years, but the Arapaho did not show up until the late 1700s.

Start: Fourth of July Trailhead at Buckingham Campground
Hiking time: About 6 hours
Distance: 6.6 miles out and back
Difficulty: Moderate
Trail surface: Dirt
Best season: Summer
Other trail users: Equestrians
Canine compatibility: Dogs are permitted on handheld, 6-foot leashes
Fees and permits: None for hiking or camping in Buckingham Campground. Permit is required for camping in Indian Peaks Wilderness

Trail contacts: USDA Forest Service, Boulder Ranger District, 2140 Yarmouth Ave., Boulder Co 80301; (303) 541-2500; fs.usda.gov/arp
Maps: Trails Illustrated Indian Peaks; USGS Monarch Lake, East Portal, Nederland
Highlights: Wildflowers, Fourth of July Mine site; views of North Fork Middle Boulder Creek valley below Mount Neva, Arapaho Pass
Wildlife: Mule deer, mountain chickadee, red squirrel
Fourth of July Trailhead elevation: 10,121 feet
Arapaho Pass elevation: 11,906 feet

Finding the Trailhead: Begin at the junction of Colorado Hwy. 72 and 119 in Nederland. From the south side of Nederland, a half mile from the joining of these highways, turn right on CR 132 toward the Lake Eldora Ski Area. Where the road forks uphill (left), stay on the lower (right) fork through the community of Eldora. Its pavement ends shortly. A mile past Eldora, the road forks again. The left fork leads to the Hessie Trailhead (high clearance vehicle recommended). The right fork climbs for a rough 4 miles to a parking area at the upper end of Buckingham Campground near the Fourth of July Trailhead. **GPS:** N39° 59' .714"/W105° 38' .052"

The Hike

At 11,906 feet, well above tree line, Arapaho Pass seems inaccurately described as a low point on the Continental Divide in Indian Peaks. Rather, it is the least high point over which to pass from Middle Park on the West Slope to Denver and Boulder on the East Slope. Therefore, in 1904, the Colorado legislature voted $5,000 to construct a road over Arapaho Pass. Even then, this was an inadequate sum, and only a broad trail ever existed, increasingly less broad as it climbed. Heading west across the pass, travelers could take trails either left or right around the flanks of Satanta Peak, named for a Kiowa warrior who fought far to the south of Colorado.

The Continental Divide dominates the view from the Arapaho Pass Trail above the valley of North Fork Middle Boulder Creek.

Mule deer fawn explores beside creek.

Arapaho Pass Trail climbs a glacier-steepened slope above North Fork Middle Boulder Creek fed by a brook crossing the path.

Arapaho Pass

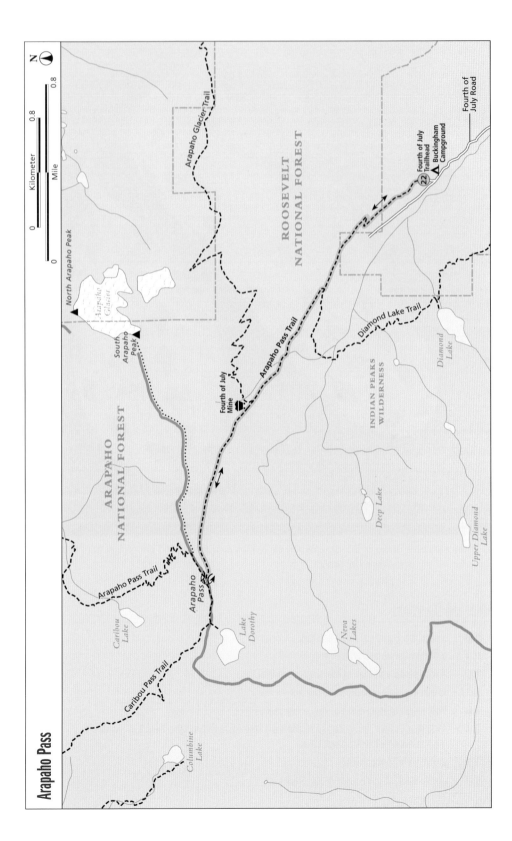

N

Kilometer
0   0.8
Mile
0   0.8

ARAPAHO NATIONAL FOREST

ROOSEVELT NATIONAL FOREST

INDIAN PEAKS WILDERNESS

North Arapaho Peak

Arapaho Glacier

South Arapaho Peak

Arapaho Glacier Trail

Fourth of July Mine

Arapaho Pass Trail

Diamond Lake Trail

Fourth of July Trailhead
22
Buckingham Campground

Fourth of July Road

Arapaho Pass Trail

Caribou Pass Trail

Caribou Lake

Arapaho Pass

Lake Dorothy

Neva Lakes

Deep Lake

Diamond Lake

Upper Diamond Lake

Columbine Lake

Arapaho moccasins in Eagle Plume collection along Colorado Highway 7 are prettier than boots but offer less protection on rocky trails.

Miles and Directions

0.0 Leave the Fourth of July Trailhead.

0.4 Enter Indian Peaks Wilderness.

1.0 Cross steep waterfall splashing across trail.

1.2 Diamond Lake Trail drops to the left.

1.8 Trail levels at the Fourth of July mine site.

2.1 Arapaho Glacier Trail ascends to the right. Ahead, note Arapaho Pass Trail slanting across ridge below Arapaho Pass.

3.3 Arrive at Arapaho Pass.

6.6 Arrive back at the Fourth of July Trailhead.

23 Lake Dorothy

Lake Dorothy is the highest named lake in Indian Peaks and is likely 100 feet deep.

Start: The Fourth of July Trailhead
Hiking time: About 6.5 hours
Distance: 7.3 out and back
Difficulty: Moderate
Trail surface: Dirt
Best season: Summer
Other trail users: Equestrians as far as Arapaho Pass. Hikers only on the spur to Lake Dorothy
Canine compatibility: Dogs are permitted on handheld, 6-foot leashes
Fees and permits: None for hiking or camping at Buckingham Campground. Permit is required for camping in Indian Peaks Wilderness

Trail contacts: USDA Forest Service, Boulder Ranger District, 2140 Yarmouth Ave., Boulder CO 80301; (303) 541-2500; fs.usda.gov/arp
Maps: Trails Illustrated Indian Peaks Gold Hill; USGS Monarch Lake, East Portal, Nederland
Highlights: Fourth of July Mine site, Arapaho Pass, Lake Dorothy, wildflowers, alpine tundra
Wildlife: Mule deer, elk, red squirrel, mountain chickadee, white-tailed ptarmigan, bighorn sheep, and even mountain goat reported.
Fourth of July Trailhead elevation: 10,121 feet
Lake Dorothy elevation: 12,061 feet

Finding the trailhead: Begin at the junction of Colorado Hwy. 72 and 119 in Nederland. From the south side of Nederland, a half mile from the joining of these highways, turn right on CR 132 toward the Lake Eldora Ski Area. Where the road forks uphill (left) toward the ski area, stay on the lower (right) fork through the community of Eldora. Its pavement ends shortly. A mile past Eldora, the road forks again. The left fork leads to the Hessie Trailhead (high clearance vehicle recommended). The right fork climbs for rough 4 miles to a parking area at the upper end of Buckingham Campground near the Fourth of July Trailhead. **GPS:** N39° 59' .714"/W105° 38' .052"

The Hike

Most likely, Lake Dorothy was named after the granddaughter of Henry Lehman, who ranched along the South Fork of the Colorado River below today's Monarch Lake Trailhead. When the family had to travel to Denver, they rode over Arapaho Pass, skirting Lake Dorothy, hanging impressively below Mount Neva. It is an easy walk from Arapaho Pass over tundra and rocks on a spur trail to Lake Dorothy.

I have named now forgotten natural features for similarly appropriate reasons. Fortunately, my names never stuck. The US Geological Survey that now approves names printed on its maps insists on a good reason for a name and usually requires that only names of dead people can be used.

Fall color comes early to tundra plants surrounding Lake Dorothy, the highest lake in Indian Peaks.

Miles and Directions

0.0   Leave from the Fourth of July Trailhead.

0.4   Enter Indian Peaks Wilderness.

1.0   Cross waterfall splashing across trail.

1.2   Diamond Lake Trail drops left.

1.8   Trail levels at Fourth of July Mine site.

2.1   Arapaho Glacier Trail ascends to the right. Ahead, note Arapaho Glacier Trail slanting across a ridge below the pass.

3.3   Arrive at Arapaho Pass. Bear left toward Lake Dorothy.

3.5   Cairn marks spur to Lake Dorothy.

3.65   Arrive at Lake Dorothy.

7.3   Arrive back at the Fourth of July Trailhead.

Dorothy Lake

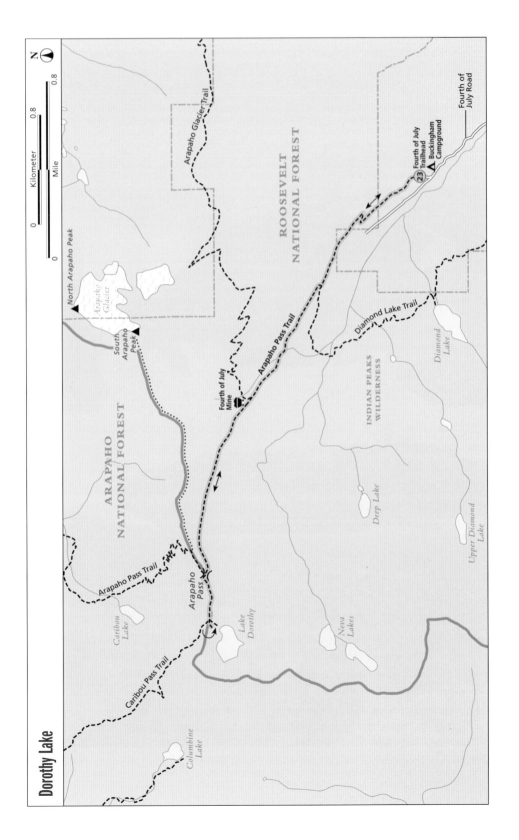

N

Kilometer
0   0.8

Mile
0   0.8

ARAPAHO
NATIONAL FOREST

ROOSEVELT
NATIONAL FOREST

North Arapaho Peak

Arapaho
Glacier

South
Arapaho
Peak

Arapaho Glacier Trail

Fourth of July
Mine

Arapaho Pass Trail

Arapaho Pass Trail

Caribou
Lake

Arapaho Pass

Caribou Pass Trail

Lake
Dorothy

Columbine
Lake

Neva
Lakes

Deep Lake

Diamond Lake Trail

Diamond
Lake

INDIAN PEAKS
WILDERNESS

Upper Diamond
Lake

Fourth of July
Trailhead

23

Buckingham
Campground

Fourth of
July Road

Mount Neva sits on the Continental Divide above Lake Dorothy.

24 South Arapaho Peak

South Arapaho presents perhaps the best views in Indian Peaks.

Start: Fourth of July Trailhead
Hiking time: About 10 hours
Distance: 8 miles out and back
Difficulty: Difficult
Trail surface: Dirt to Arapaho Glacier overlook; boulders thereafter to the summit
Best season: Summer
Other trail users: Equestrians on Arapaho Pass Trail
Canine compatibility: Dogs are permitted on handheld 6-foot leashes
Fees and permits: None for hiking or for camping at Buckingham Campground. Permit required to camp in Indian Peaks Wilderness

Trail contacts: USDA Forest Service, Boulder Ranger District, 2140 Yarmouth Ave., Boulder CO 80301; (303) 541-2500; fs.usda.gov/arp
Maps: Trails Illustrated Indian Peaks Gold Hill; USGS Monarch Lake, East Portal, Nederland
Highlights: Fourth of July Mine site, wildflowers, Arapaho Glacier overlook, South Arapaho Peak
Wildlife: Mule Deer, red squirrel, pika, yellow-bellied marmot, mountain chickadee.
Fourth of July Trailhead elevation: 10,121 feet
South Arapaho Peak elevation: 13,397 feet

Finding the trailhead: Begin at junction of Colorado Hwy. 72 and 119 in Nederland. From the south side of Nederland a half mile from the joining of these highways, turn right on CR 132 toward the Lake Eldora Ski Area. Where the road forks uphill (left) toward the ski area, stay on the lower fork through the community of Eldora. Its pavement ends shortly. A mile past Eldora, the road forks again. The left fork leads to the Hessie Trailhead (high clearance vehicle recommended). The right fork climbs for a rough 4 miles to a parking area at the upper end of Buckingham Campground near the Fourth of July Trailhead. **GPS:** N39° 59' .714"/W105° 38' .052"

The Hike

From the Fourth of July Trailhead, the Arapaho Pass Trail maintains a consistent grade along the steep north wall of North Fork Middle Boulder Creek valley. Subalpine wildflowers hugging the trail are very lovely, and the slope is so steep above and below that hikers are looking either at flowers at eye level or down to tall flowers blooming at boot level. The view up the valley to Mount Neva is extremely impressive. For a short stretch at the Fourth of July Mine site, the trail levels. Soon a branch climbs steeply right from the Arapaho Pass Trail through switchbacks to the Arapaho Glacier overlook. A more gradual ascent to the overlook follows the Arapaho Glacier Trail from Rainbow Lakes Campground. Of course, more gradual means longer (twice as long) than via the tight switchbacks rising from the Arapaho Pass Trail.

Above the overlook of Arapaho Glacier, there is no path. A puff-and-pant from boulder to boulder up the south ridge to South Arapaho's summit is not technically difficult or scary. What is somewhat daunting is imagining how devoted mountaineers

Glacier-carved cliffs dominate the view south from the summit of South Arapaho Peak.

A yellow-bellied marmot grazes on alpine avens, an abundant tundra plant on South Arapaho Peak.

South Arapaho Peak

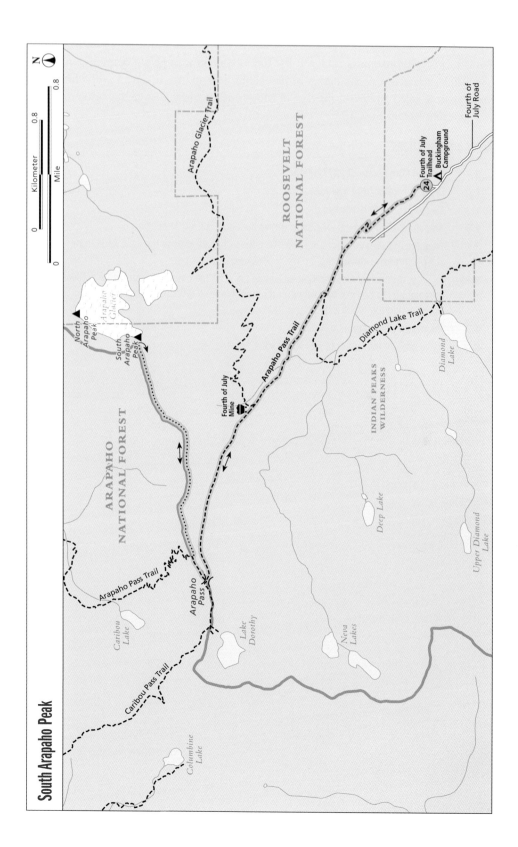

N

Kilometer
0   0.8

Mile
0   0.8

ARAPAHO
NATIONAL FOREST

ROOSEVELT
NATIONAL FOREST

INDIAN PEAKS
WILDERNESS

North
Arapaho
Peak

Arapaho
Glacier

South
Arapaho
Peak

Arapaho Glacier Trail

Arapaho Pass Trail

Diamond Lake Trail

Fourth of July
Mine

Fourth of July
Trailhead

Buckingham
Campground

Fourth of
July Road

24

Arapaho Pass Trail

Caribou Pass Trail

Arapaho Pass

Caribou
Lake

Columbine
Lake

Lake
Dorothy

Neva
Lakes

Deep Lake

Upper Diamond
Lake

Diamond
Lake

hauled a heavy bronze peak finder to the top to cement it in place. Squinting across the plate's surface reveals the names of mountains near and far as distant as the intersecting, snow-filled gullies on the face of Mount of the Holy Cross, Colorado's most recognizable 14,000-foot peak.

Miles and Directions

0.0   Set out from Fourth of July Trailhead.

1.0   Cross a waterfall that splashes across the trail.

1.2   Diamond Lake Trail drops to the left.

1.8   Arapaho Pass Trail levels for a short way at the Fourth of July Mine site.

2.1   From the Arapaho Pass Trail, the Arapaho Glacier Trail ascends to the right, soon rising steeply through switchbacks.

2.85   Arrive at overlook of Arapaho Glacier and end of a visible path up South Arapaho. Climb from boulder to boulder over whatever route seems least laborious, always up toward the assumed top of the peak.

4.0   Top out on South Arapaho Peak.

8.0   Arrive back at the Fourth of July Trailhead.

25 North Arapaho Peak

This ascent to the tallest summit in Indian Peaks (more than 4,000 meters, which is important to some peak baggers) can be scary and requires great care though no technical climbing equipment (a rope in the hands of a competent leader may make some climbers feel calmer).

Start: Fourth of July Trailhead
Hiking time: About 11 hours
Distance: 9 miles out and back
Difficulty: Difficult
Trail surface: Dirt as far as overlook of Arapaho Glacier, then rock
Best season: Summer
Other trail users: Equestrians on Arapaho Pass Trail
Canine compatibility: Dogs are permitted on handheld, 6-foot leads, but this summit is not dog friendly because dogs lack grasping thumbs that humans find reassuring to climb North Arapaho. I am the last one to say it, but for this ascent leave the dogs behind

Fees and permits: None for hiking or camping in Buckingham Campground. Permit is required for camping in Indian Peaks Wilderness
Trail contacts: USDA Forest Service, Boulder Ranger District, 2140 Yarmouth Ave., Boulder CO 80301; (303) 541-2500; fs.usda.gov/arp
Maps: Trails Illustrated Indian Peaks Gold Hill; USGS Monarch Lake, East Portal, Nederland
Highlights: Fourth of July Mine site; Arapaho Glacier overlook, South Arapaho Peak, North Arapaho Peak
Wildlife: Mule deer, red squirrel, mountain chickadee, yellow-bellied marmot, pika
Fourth of July Trailhead elevation: 10,121 feet
North Arapaho Peak elevation: 13,502 feet

Finding the trailhead: Begin at the junction of Colorado Hwy. 72 and 119 in Nederland. From the south side of Nederland, a half mile from the joining of these highways, turn right on CR 132 toward the Lake Eldora Ski Area. Where the road forks uphill (left) toward the ski area, stay on the lower (right) fork through the community of Eldora. Its pavement ends shortly. A mile past Eldora, the road forks again. The left fork leads to the Hessie Trailhead (high clearance vehicle recommended). The right fork climbs for a rough 4 miles to a parking area at the upper end of Buckingham Campground near the Fourth of July Trailhead. **GPS:** N39° 59' .714"/W105° 38' .052"

The Hike

North Arapaho is the tallest of the Indian Peaks. And it is somewhat more challenging than its neighbor to the south.

The most efficient way to climb North Arapaho Peak is to begin at the Fourth of July Trailhead and ascend the Arapaho Pass Trail as far as the Fourth of July Mine site. On the way, the trail clings to the north wall of the U-shaped valley of North Fork Middle Boulder Creek, steepened to a near vertical orientation by the passing of mountain glaciers in geological waves extending from many millennia to as recently as 10,000 years ago. During the current warm centuries, the wall displays masses of grass and flowers.

Arapaho Glacier hangs beneath South and North Arapaho peaks.

Rosettes of big-rooted spring beauty turns bright red in fall.

At the rusted rubble marking the more level Fourth of July Mine site, the trail splits. Arapaho Pass Trail continues west where the Arapaho Glacier Trail cuts sharply right. Taking the right branch, hikers soon encounter much steeper terrain climbed by switchbacks to an overlook of Arapaho Glacier. After reaching the overlook, the path ends to be followed by a rugged, but not frightening trudge from boulder to boulder, stair stepping to the summit of South Arapaho Peak.

The half mile to the summit of North Arapaho is more exciting. Descend north to the saddle between the Arapahos, a climb as uncomplicated as the ascent from the glacier overlook, but perhaps more subject to falling. Proceeding to North Arapaho involves real climbing over rocks exposed to high cliffs. Splotches of red paint mark the least hazardous route, but can be disguised in fall by abundant splotches of red marking the leaves of big-rooted spring beauty rosettes. Though not a technical route requiring rock-climbing gear, the way up North Arapaho may seem less fearsome for some folks if they are belayed by a rope in the hands of a competent leader. A rope may seem like an unnecessary burden, but consider that preceding climbers hauled a bronze peak finder up South Arapaho and a container of paint to mark the rocks on scary North Arapaho. In any case, all climbers, novice or experienced, need to be cautious.

Atop North Arapaho is a further monument to the willingness of some mountaineers to engage in extra work. A huge cairn (pile of rocks) marks the summit and is large enough to seat a complete climbing party, yet several feet higher atop Indian

North Arapaho Peak

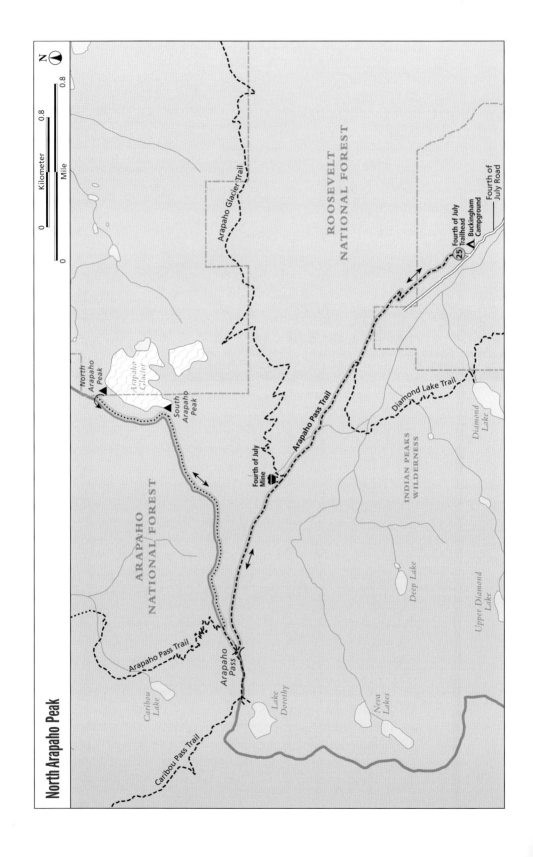

N

Kilometer
0   0.8

Mile
0   0.8

ARAPAHO
NATIONAL FOREST

ROOSEVELT
NATIONAL FOREST

INDIAN PEAKS
WILDERNESS

North
Arapaho
Peak

Arapaho Glacier
South
Arapaho
Peak

Arapaho Glacier Trail

Diamond Lake Trail

Fourth of July
Mine

Arapaho Pass Trail

Arapaho Pass Trail

Arapaho
Pass

Caribou Pass Trail

Caribou
Lake

Lake Dorothy

Neva
Lakes

Deep Lake

Upper Diamond
Lake

Diamond
Lake

Fourth of July
Trailhead

25

Buckingham
Campground

Fourth of
July Road

Peaks highest mountain. (I wonder if this structure was a survey point visible to record mining claims in the valleys below.)

The summit cairn is not high enough to substantially improve the view. But substantial improvement can be achieved by moving lower to a prominence a bit south of the summit. Here, the view of climbers atop an absolutely sheer cliff above Arapaho Glacier is very impressive when viewed from the true summit; the climbers do not have to be near the edge to make the composition work. Although the danger is not as real as it appears, take care. Rock steady may be a conflict in terms as geological forces constantly erode the height of North Arapaho Peak. And vertigo (sudden dizziness) has sent experienced mountain climbers worldwide over the edges of a multitude of cliffs.

Miles and Directions

0.0	Boldly depart from Fourth of July Trailhead on the Arapaho Pass Trail.
1.0	Cross a steep waterfall splashing across the trail.
1.2	Diamond Lake Trail drops to the left. Continue up the Arapaho Pass Trail.
1.8	Arapaho Pass Trail becomes less steep for a short distance where rusted equipment marks the site of the Fourth of July Mine.
2.1	Climb right on Arapaho Glacier Trail.
2.85	Reach the overlook of Arapaho Glacier. Begin stair step trudge up pathless route to the top of South Arapaho Peak.
4.0	Top out on summit of South Arapaho. Begin stair step descent to the saddle between the Arapahos.
4.5	Arrive on the summit of North Arapaho.
9.0	Arrive back at the Fourth of July Trailhead.

26 Caribou Pass

Caribou Pass is west of the Continental Divide and is described in the West Slope section account of climbing Satanta Peak (Hike 44). But, the trail from Arapaho Pass in the direction of Caribou Pass is so dramatic that it needs to be experienced by hikers approaching from the east, if snow is not blocking it.

Start: Fourth of July Trailhead
Hiking time: About 7 hours
Distance: 8 miles out and back
Difficulty: Moderate
Trail surface: Dirt
Best season: Summer
Other trail users: Equestrians on Arapaho Pass Trail
Canine compatibility: Dogs are permitted on handheld, 6-foot leashes
Fees and permits: None when leaving from Fourth of July Trailhead, a fee when leaving from Junco Lake Trailhead on West Slope. No fee required for camping at Buckingham Campground. Camping within Indian Peaks Wilderness requires permit

Trail contacts: USDA Forest Service, Boulder Ranger District, 2140 Yarmouth Ave., Boulder CO 80301; (303) 541-2500; fs.usda.gov/arp, or Sulphur Ranger District, P. O. Box 10, 9 Ten Mile Dr., Granby CO 80466; (970) 887-4100; fs.usda.gov/arp
Maps: Trails Illustrated Indian Peaks Gold Hill; USGS Monarch Lake, East Portal, Nederland
Highlights: Wildflowers, Fourth of July Mine site, alpine tundra, Arapaho Pass, Lake Dorothy, Caribou Pass Trail, Caribou Pass
Wildlife: Mule deer, chipmunk, red squirrel, yellow-bellied marmot, mountain chickadee, pika
Fourth of July Trailhead elevation: 10,121 feet
Caribou Pass elevation: 11,851 feet

Finding the trailhead: Begin at the junction of Colorado Hwy. 72 and 119 in Nederland. From the south side of Nederland, a half mile from the joining of these highways, turn right on CR 132 toward the Lake Eldora Ski Area. Where the road forks uphill (left), stay on the lower fork (right) through the community of Eldora. Its pavement ends shortly. A mile past Eldora, the road forks again. The left fork leads to the Hessie Trailhead (high clearance vehicle recommended). The right fork climbs for rough 4 miles to a parking area at the upper end of Buckingham Campground near the Fourth of July Trailhead. **GPS:** N59° 59' .714"/W105° 38' .052"

The Hike

If you see a caribou (reindeer) at Caribou Pass, presume that lack of oxygen at high altitude has fogged your brain badly and retreat to tree line. Although the name Caribou attached to every conceivable geographic formation is scattered across an Indian Peaks map, Santa Claus never could have recruited his most noteworthy draft animals here. A nineteenth-century prospector thought the mining region around Indian Peaks looked like a Canadian mining region where there really were caribou. Therefore, he named his tons of silver mining interests Caribou, and the name spread like a rumor of a new gold strike in a Central City bar.

The Caribou Pass Trail is a thin line across the cliff at the head of Arapaho Creek valley.

Caribou do not dwell in Colorado wilderness areas even though their name is common on Indian Peaks maps.

Caribou Pass is accessible from Arapaho Pass along an easy-to-walk old wagon road, thinned by erosion in places to trail width. Although the views are typically Indian Peaks gorgeous, the main attraction is the road itself where it is cut from a cliff far above Caribou Lake. As mentioned in the introductory section on geology, my favorite terminal and recessional moraines, perhaps only 1,000 years old hang below the pass and road.

Miles and Directions

0.0   Depart from Fourth of July Trailhead on the Arapaho Pass Trail.

0.4   Enter Indian Peaks Wilderness.

1.0   Cross a steep waterfall splashing across the Arapaho Pass Trail.

1.2   Diamond Lake Trail drops to the left. Continue on the Arapaho Pass Trial.

1.8   Encounter rusted equipment marking the site of 1872 Fourth of July Mine.

2.1   Arapaho Glacier Trail cuts right from Arapaho Pass Trail. Continue on Arapaho Pass Trail to where it climbs diagonally across a ridge to the pass.

3.3   Arrive at Arapaho Pass. Head left.

3.5   Cairn marks spur trail to Lake Dorothy, easy 0.15 mile from Caribou Pass Trail.

3.7   An old (now narrowed by erosion) wagon road cuts dramatically across a broad cliff approximately 750 feet above Caribou Lake. This route is described by the Forest Service as "not for the faint of heart." It also might be described as a field test for acrophobia.

4.0   Arrive at Caribou Pass.

8.0   Arrive back at the Fourth of July Trailhead.

Caribou Pass

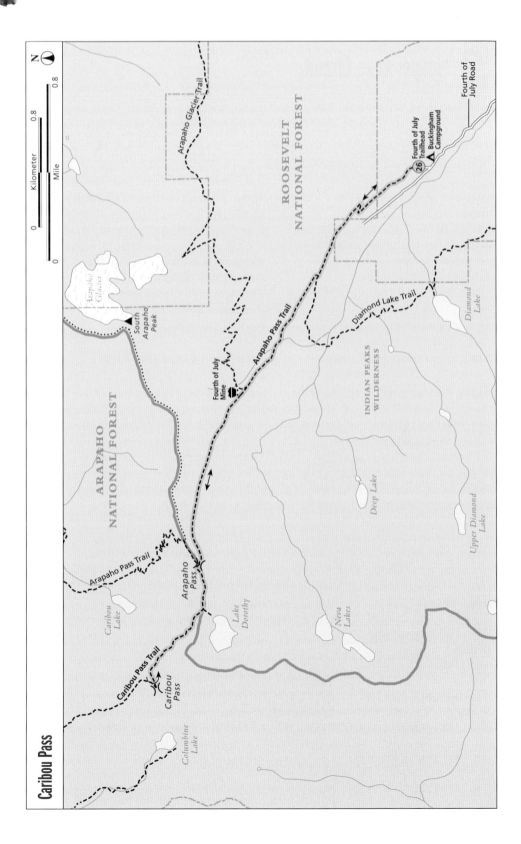

N

Kilometer
0   0.8

Mile
0   0.8

ARAPAHO
NATIONAL FOREST

Arapaho Glacier Trail

Arapaho Glacier

South
Arapaho
Peak

Arapaho Pass Trail

Caribou
Lake

Arapaho Pass Trail

Arapaho
Pass

Caribou Pass Trail

Caribou
Pass

Columbine
Lake

Lake
Dorothy

Fourth of July Mine

ROOSEVELT
NATIONAL FOREST

Diamond Lake Trail

Fourth of July
Trailhead

26

Buckingham
Campground

Fourth of
July Road

INDIAN PEAKS
WILDERNESS

Deep Lake

Neva
Lakes

Upper Diamond
Lake

Diamond
Lake

27 Jasper Lake Circuit

Jasper Lake is a reservoir with a barely noticeable dam and sometimes barely notice-able water. Normally, its three obvious forested shores and glacier-carved ridge, rising to the north, proclaim that frozen water in the distant past was always present.

Start: Fourth of July Trailhead

Hiking time: About 9 hours

Distance: 10.5 miles circuit

Trail surface: Dirt most of the way, until foot bashing cobbles take over on the way down

Best season: Summer

Other trail users: Equestrians

Canine compatibility: Dogs are permitted on handheld, 6-foot leashes

Fees and permits: None for hiking or camping in Buckingham Campground. Permit is required for camping in Indian Peaks Wilderness

Trail contacts: USDA Forest Service, Boulder Ranger District, 2140 Yarmouth Ave., Boulder CO 80301; (303) 541-2500; fs.usda.gov/arp

Maps: Trails Illustrated Indian Peaks Gold Hill; USGS Monarch Lake, East Portal, Nederland

Highlights: Wildflowers, North Fork Middle Boulder Creek, Diamond Lake, Jasper Lake

Wildlife: Mule deer, red squirrel, mountain chickadee, chipmunk, moose, beaver

Fourth of July Trailhead elevation: 10,121 feet

Jasper Lake elevation: 10,814 feet

Finding the trailhead: The first part of the road begin at junction of Colorado Hwy. 72 and 119 in Nederland. From the south edge of Nederland, half a mile from the joining of these highways, turn right on CR 116, toward Lake Eldora Ski Area. Where the road forks uphill (left) stay on the lower fork and continue through the community of Eldora. Its pavement ends shortly. A mile past Eldora, the road forks again. The left fork leads on to a cobbled road rough enough to discourage use of normal passenger cars, which can be parked along the south edge of the road from Eldora. (High clearance vehicles can proceed about a quarter mile to the Hessie Trailhead where there is limited parking) **GPS:** N39° 57' .1"/W105° 35' .696".

The right fork climbs the first part of this road may be flooded, but a trail has been built along the right side to lift hikers above the worst parts. The right fork climbs for a rough 4 miles to the upper end of Buckingham Campground near the Fourth of July Trailhead. Begin hiking at Fourth of July Trailhead and end alongside the road east of the fork. **GPS:** N39° 59' .714"/ W105° 38' .052"

The Hike

Glaciers, millennia ago, sculpted U-shaped valleys in Indian Peaks, separated by steep-sided and high ridges. Visually appealing as this topography is, it does pose some navi-gational problems for hikers seeking to walk from one valley to another. Thus, most of the trails described in this guide extend in and out on the same route, often trending east and west. So rich in interest and scenery are all of these trails that most folks find pleasing variety in hiking them twice, once in each direction.

Dead trees float to the south shore near Jasper Lake's outlet creek.

Nonetheless, the occasional loop or circuit hike is highly valued. By using two vehicles to shuttle hikers between Fourth of July Trailhead and 4-mile-distant Hessie Trailhead, such a loop trip is possible with only 1.2 miles of step-retracing along a lovely circuit of trails.

Begin at Fourth of July Trailhead, after depositing a vehicle at Hessie Trailhead for use in retrieving the vehicle left at Buckingham. The narrow Arapaho Pass Trail clings to a steep slope amid wildflowers accenting views across the valley below Mount Neva, named for a nineteenth-century Arapaho. A little more than a mile from the trailhead, a branch left descends for a half mile to a particularly scenic crossing of North Fork Middle Boulder Creek, complete with wildflowers and waterfall. The next mile to Diamond Lake is extremely pleasant through thick subalpine forest opened by flowery marshes.

The trailside delights multiply beyond Diamond Lake amid likely the best wildflower display in Indian Peaks with South Arapaho Peak rising above, a floral extravaganza scarcely diminished as the trail rises over an alpine tundra-covered ridge. About 2.3 miles from Diamond Lake, the trail intersects the route to Jasper Lake, a reservoir about 0.6 mile west (right) from the junction.

From the lake, you can begin to close the loop toward Hessie Trailhead by retracing your steps to the Diamond Lake Trail and continuing to the fork between the Devils Thumb Trail and the Devils Thumb Bypass Trail. Go left along the bypass; if you sleep walk beyond it and encounter Jasper Creek, turn around and go back to the bypass to stay north of the creek through meadows and past the wilderness boundary to rejoin the Devils Thumb Trail a few steps from a bridge across the creek. Turn left away from the bridge to continue downhill on a 4WD road used for Jasper Lake maintenance. As is typical on such routes, the 4WD traffic has filled the trail with cobbles that are not gentle on even booted feet. About 0.6 miles of stumbling and sliding (better when going downhill than up) leads to Hessie Trailhead. A quarter mile of cobbled road leads to the road fork where 2WD vehicles wait for hikers' return.

If you do not have a second car available for shuttle purposes, you can scrap the loop concept and return to Fourth of July Trailhead at Buckingham Campground by the way you reached Jasper Lake. This is one-third mile further in each direction than beginning at Fourth of July Trailhead, but the more rewarding trail is worth the greater distance.

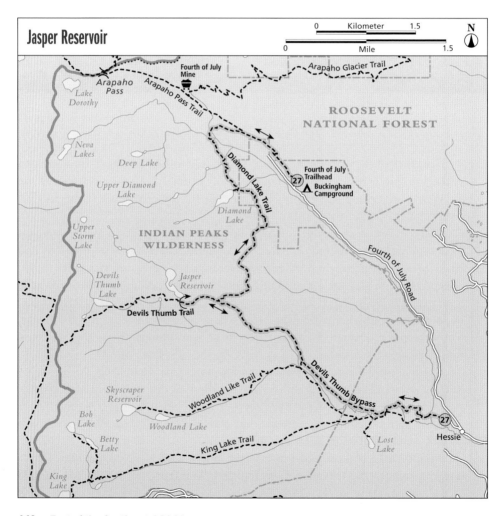

Jasper Reservoir

Miles and Directions

0.0 Leave on the Arapaho Pass Trail from the Fourth of July Trailhead at Buckingham Campground.

0.4 Enter Indian Peaks Wilderness.

1.0 Cross a steep waterfall that splashes across the trail.

1.2 Leave the Arapaho Pass Trail, dropping left on the Diamond Lake Trail.

1.7 Traverse North Fork Middle Boulder Creek at an exceptionally lovely stream crossing.

2.8 Arrive at Diamond Lake. Continue past incredible wildflower gardens (yes, even better than you already have passed) for 2.35 miles to meet Devils Thumb Trail (4WD road to Jasper Lake).

5.15 Turn right on Devils Thumb Trail.

5.75 Arrive at Jasper Lake.

6.05 Retrace your steps down Devils Thumb Trail to the Diamond Lake Trail. Watch for moose and beaver among willows lining Jasper Creek. Assuming you have shuttle car in place, continue down the Devils Thumb Trail to follow the Devils Thumb Bypass Trail north of Jasper Creek.

7.07 Bear left on Devils Thumb Bypass Trail.

8.12 Leave Indian Peaks Wilderness.

9.75 Rejoin the Devils Thumb Trail (4WD road) a few steps below a bridge. Turn left away from the bridge.

10.25 Cross bridge to Hessie Trailhead.

10.5 Arrive back at fork in road to pick up your shuttle car.

28 Devils Thumb Lake

Devils Thumb Lake is named for a sharp rock spire that dominates the slope above the lake.

Start: Hessie Trailhead
Hiking time: About 9 hours
Distance: 10.9 miles out and back
Difficulty: Moderate
Trail surface: Dirt
Best season: Summer
Other trail users: Equestrians
Canine compatibility: Dogs are permitted on handheld, 6-foot leashes
Fees and permits: None for hiking. Permit is required for camping in Indian Peaks Wilderness

Trail contacts: USDA Forest Service, Boulder Ranger District, 2140 Yarmouth Ave., Boulder CO 80301; (303) 541-2500; fs.usda.gov/arp
Maps: Trails Illustrated Indian Peaks Gold Hill; USGS Monarch Lake, East Portal, Nederland
Highlights: Wildflowers, Jasper Lake, Devils Thumb Lake
Wildlife: Mule deer, red squirrel, mountain chickadee
Hessie Trailhead elevation: 9,009 feet
Devils Thumb Lake elevation: 11,140 feet

Finding the trailhead: Begin at the junction of Colorado Hwy. 72 and 119 in Nederland. From the south side of Nederland, a half mile from the joining of these highways, turn right on CR 132 toward the Lake Eldora Ski Area. Where the road forks uphill (left) toward the ski area, stay on the lower (right) fork through the community of Eldora. Its pavement ends shortly. A mile past Eldora, the road forks again. Normal passenger vehicles lacking high clearance should turn around at this fork to park in locations along the south side of the road marked by signs. **GPS:** N39° 57' .1"/W105° 35' .696"

The Hessie Trailhead is a quarter mile along a road/creek bed that sometimes carries water and always is paved by cobbles hard on even booted feet. The worst parts are bordered by a trail that lifts hikers above this hassle. High clearance vehicles can make it all the way to the Hessie Trailhead and less-than-abundant parking. A bridge carries hikers across North Fork Middle Boulder Creek. Rather ironic signs near the bridge prohibit vehicles from splashing across the creek and also prohibit parking at a spot blocking an obvious vehicle ford. Across the bridge, hikers follow a distressingly rocky road used for reservoir maintenance high in Indian Peaks Wilderness.

The Hike

The route to Devils Thumb Lake from the east begins at Hessie Trailhead. A shorter route from the west begins at Rollins Pass; described in Hike 46, Devils Thumb Pass. From Hessie (the site of a disappeared mining town), follow a rocky service road (Devils Thumb Trail) for about a 0.6 mile to a right turn at the Devils Thumb Bypass Trail, If you come to a second bridge, you have gone a few steps too far. The bypass trail, which climbs along the right bank of Jasper Creek, is shorter and easier on the feet than the Devils Thumb Trail.

Devils Thumb Lake catches a flood of rocks on its north shore.

About 1.5 miles after the bypass, rejoins the Devils Thumb Trail, the Diamond Lake Trail arrives from the right (see Hike 27, Jasper Lake Circuit). From the Diamond Lake Trail junction, another 0.6 miles takes you to Jasper Lake. If the water has not been drained away for nonscenic purposes, the lake is justifiably popular for its forest-and-cliff-rimmed vistas. Beyond Jasper Lake, a mile-long stroll takes you to Devils Thumb Lake, with a good view of the thumb and krummholz (twisted wood) trees along the trail.

Tree line dips rather low at Devils Thumb Lake, at least on the thumb side where a flood of rock wedged from a ridge extending east from the Continental Divide runs down to the lake's edge, providing no chance for trees to grow. On the contrastingly level valley floor, however, the trail reaches the shore at tree line defined by trees much miniaturized by weather. Several switchbacks climb the steep side of a ridge to surmount the Continental Divide; snow and ice can complicate this path until late July.

Miles and Directions

0.0   Park 2WD vehicles on the south side of the road west of Eldora. Walk to Hessie Trailhead.

0.25 From Hessie Trailhead, cross North Fork Middle Boulder Creek on a bridge.

0.85 Devils Thumb Bypass Trail cuts sharply right a few yards short of a second bridge. Follow the bypass.

1.4   Cross Indian Peaks Wilderness boundary.

2.2   Walk past the trail to Woodland Lake, which cuts back sharply to the left.

4.5   Arrive at Jasper Lake.

5.5   Arrive at Devils Thumb Lake.

11.0 Arrive back at the fork in road west of Eldora.

Devils Thumb perches above wildflowers near Devils Thumb Lake.

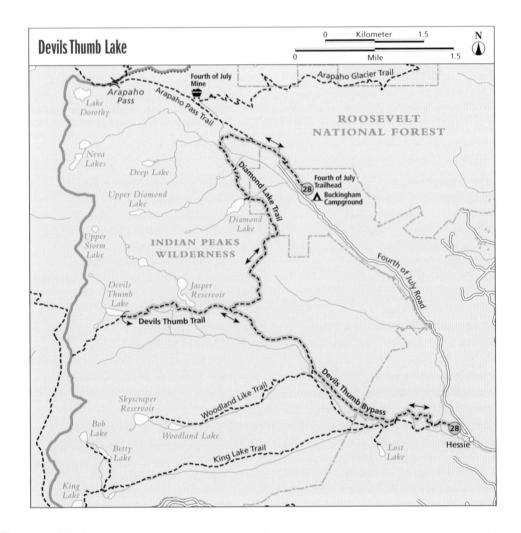

Kilometer 1.5

Mile 1.5

N

ROOSEVELT
NATIONAL FOREST

Fourth of July
Mine

Arapaho Glacier Trail

Lake
Dorothy

Arapaho
Pass

Arapaho Pass Trail

Neva
Lakes

Deep Lake

Diamond Lake Trail

Fourth of July
Trailhead

28

Buckingham
Campground

Upper Diamond
Lake

Diamond
Lake

Upper
Storm
Lake

INDIAN PEAKS
WILDERNESS

Fourth of July Road

Devils
Thumb
Lake

Jasper
Reservoir

Devils Thumb Trail

Skyscraper
Reservoir

Woodland Like Trail

Devils Thumb Bypass

28

Bob
Lake

Woodland Lake

Lost
Lake

Hessie

Betty
Lake

King Lake Trail

King
Lake

THE DEVIL

So many natural features have been named for the devil, that it seems his anatomy could be reconstructed from American geology. For instance, west of Loveland, Colorado, US Hwy. 34 passes Devils Backbone, presumably a more important body part than his thumb. The most famous advocate for wilderness values, John Muir, took light-hearted exception to giving credit to the devil for what Muir considered to be God's most wonderful creations. Muir wrote of high mountain formations "far above the region usually haunted by the devil; for though we read that he once climbed an exceedingly high mountain, he cannot be much of a mountaineer, for his tracks are seldom seen above the timberline." Muir presumed that his readers would recognize his biblical reference to the temptation of Jesus by the devil. This presumption may be no longer valid, and Muir's reference is to the fourth chapter, eighth verse of *Matthew*'s gospel.

29 Woodland Lake

Wildflower splendor on the way to Woodland Lake is exceeded by the Diamond Lake Trail only because South Arapaho Peak soars above the Diamond Lake flowers. Up close, the Woodland Lake flowers inspire tears of admiration.

Start: Hessie Trailhead
Hiking time: About 7 hours
Distance: 8.6 miles out and back
Difficulty: Moderate
Trail surface: Dirt
Best season: Summer
Other trail users: Equestrians
Canine compatibility: Dogs are permitted on heldheld, 6-foot leashes
Fees and permits: None for hiking. Permit required for camping in Indian Peaks Wilderness

Trail contacts: USDA Forest Service, Boulder Ranger District, 2140 Yarmouth Ave., Boulder CO 80301; (303) 541-2500; fs.usda.gov/arp
Maps: Trails Illustrated Indian Peaks Gold Hill; USGS East Portal, Nederland
Highlights: Wildflowers, whitewater creeks, Woodland Lake
Wildlife: Mule deer, elk, red squirrel, mountain chickadee, dusky grouse
Hessie Trailhead elevation: 9,006 feet
Woodland Lake elevation: 10,972 feet

Finding the trailhead: Begin at the junction of Colorado Hwy. 72 and 119 in Nederland. From the south side of Nederland, a half mile from the joining of these highways, turn right on CR 132 toward the Lake Eldora Ski Area. Where the road forks uphill (left) toward the ski area, stay on the lower (right) fork through the community of Eldora. Its pavement ends shortly. A mile past Eldora, the road forks again. Normal passenger vehicles lacking high clearance should turn around at this fork to park in locations along the south side of the road marked by signs. The Hessie Trailhead is a quarter mile along a road/creek bed that sometimes carries water and always is paved by cobbles hard on even booted feet. The worst parts are bordered by a trail that lifts hikers above this hassle. High clearance vehicles can make it all the way to the Hessie Trailhead (**GPS:** N39° 57' .1"/ W105° 35' .696") and less-than-abundant parking. A bridge carries hikers across North Fork Middle Boulder Creek. Rather ironic signs near the bridge prohibit vehicles from splashing across the creek and also prohibit parking at a spot blocking an obvious vehicle ford. Across the bridge, hikers follow a distressingly rocky road used for reservoir maintenance high in Indian Peaks Wilderness.

The Hike

What the Devils Thumb Bypass does not pass by is the trail to Woodland Lake. After crossing a footbridge over North Fork Middle Boulder Creek, a road of rocks climbs fairly steeply for 0.6 mile to the bypass at another bridge, this one over South Fork Middle Boulder Creek. Cross the bridge and enjoy water music along the Devils Thumb Trail that swells to a double forte at a falls gushing through a rock chute. Some locals call it Hessie Falls.

About a half mile from the bridge, stay right on the Devils Thumb Trail where the Lost Lake Trail goes left. Another 0.2 miles brings hikers to the King Lake Trail

A wide variety of wildflowers, including harebell (blue), Indian paintbrush (red and yellow), bistort (white), chiming bells (blue), cow parsnip and angelica (large, white, composite blooms), and yellow composites (often called "DYCs" by hikers who find find distinguishing the yellow composites troublesome) are abundant along Woodland Creek.

Woodland Creek waters spectacular wildflower displays along the trail to Woodland Lake.

Dusky grouse hen and chick explore Indian Peaks forest.

junction. Again, go right and enter Indian Peaks Wilderness just beyond the junction. Another semi-level mile leads to the Woodland Lake Trail junction. Head left to climb a much steeper grade along a creek before leveling again. Woodland Lake is about 2 miles ahead, but getting there is delayed by the need to stop and at least admire if not smell the blossoms along the way. The trail may be sloppy. Slop through the mud rather than contribute to a web of trails sacrificing glorious vegetation.

Miles and Directions

0.0   Park normal passenger vehicles on south side of the road where it forks to Buckingham Campground and Hessie Trailhead. Walk to Hessie Trailhead.

0.25   If you have a high clearance vehicle, park in one of the few spaces at Hessie Trailhead.

0.85   Devils Thumb Bypass Trail heads right a few steps before a bridge. Cross the bridge on the Devils Thumb Trail.

1.35   Lost Lake Trail heads left. Continue on right fork.

1.55   King Lake Trail heads left. Continue on right fork.

2.55   Woodland Lake Trail heads left from Devils Thumb Trail.

4.3   Arrive at Woodland Lake.

8.6   Return to Hessie Trailhead.

8.85   Arrive back at your parked car.

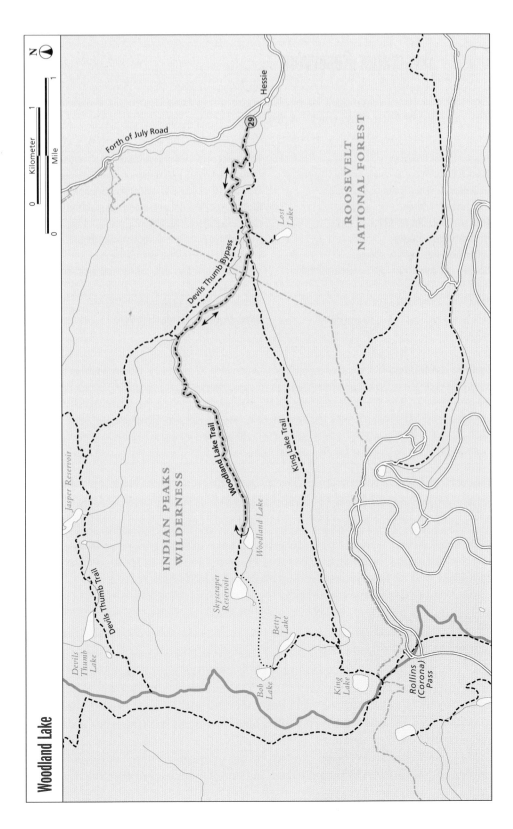

Woodland Lake

Kilometer

Mile

Forth of July Road

Hessie

29

Devils Thumb Bypass

Lost
Lake

ROOSEVELT
NATIONAL FOREST

INDIAN PEAKS
WILDERNESS

Jasper Reservoir

Woodland Lake Trail

King Lake Trail

Devils Thumb Trail

Skyscraper
Reservoir

Woodland Lake

Betty
Lake

Devils
Thumb
Lake

Bob
Lake

King
Lake

Rollins
(Corona
Pass)

30 Skyscraper Reservoir

Aptly named for its altitude, Skyscraper Reservoir boasts an interesting rock masonry dam over which water flows when the reservoir is at capacity.

Start: Hessie Trailhead
Hiking time: About 8 hours
Distance: 9.6 miles out and back
Difficulty: Moderate
Trail surface: Dirt and rock
Best season: Summer
Other trail users: Equestrians
Canine compatibility: Dogs are permitted on handheld, 6-foot leash
Fees and permits: None for hiking. Permit is required for camping in Indian Peaks Wilderness

Trail contacts: USDA Forest Service, Boulder Ranger District, 2140 Yarmouth Ave., Boulder CO 80301; (303) 541-2500; fs.usda.gov/arp
Maps: Trails Illustrated Indian Peaks Gold Hill, USGS East Portal, Nederland
Highlights: Wildflowers, whitewater streams, Woodland Lake, Skyscraper Reservoir
Wildlife: Mule deer, elk, red squirrel, mountain chickadee
Hessie Trailhead elevation: 9,006 feet
Skyscraper Reservoir elevation: 11,221 feet

Finding the trailhead: Begin at the junction of Colorado Hwy. 72 and 119 in Nederland. From the south side of Nederland, a half mile from the joining of these highways, turn right on CR 132 toward the Lake Eldora Ski Area. Where the road forks uphill (left) toward the ski area, stay on the lower (right) fork through the community of Eldora. Its pavement ends shortly. A mile past Eldora, the road forks again. Normal passenger vehicles lacking high clearance should turn around at this fork to park in locations along the south side of the road marked by signs. GPS: N39° 57' .1"/W105° 35' .696"

The Hessie Trailhead is a quarter mile along a road/creek bed that sometimes carries water and always is paved by cobbles hard on even booted feet. The worst parts are bordered by a trail that lifts hikers above this hassle. High clearance vehicles can make it all the way to the Hessie Trailhead and less-than-abundant parking. A bridge carries hikers across North Fork Middle Boulder Creek. Rather ironic signs near the bridge prohibit vehicles from splashing across the creek and also prohibit parking at a spot blocking an obvious vehicle ford. Across the bridge, hikers follow a distressingly rocky road used for reservoir maintenance high in Indian Peaks Wilderness.

The Hike

Built between 1941 and 1947, the 24-foot dam creating Skyscraper Reservoir displays artistic masonry of rock presumably gathered at the site. Originally intended to be irrigation water, the reservoir was sold to the thirsty city of Boulder in 1966. Contained in a classic glacial cirque, it seems unusual that this bowl needed human alteration to create a lake that such cirques often contain. If hikers ignore the dam, the reservoir looks very natural.

Skyscraper Reservoir is held in place by an arch dam of stone and concrete, substances capable of withstanding a huge amount of compression. Were the dam a

Skyscraper Reservoir sits in the rock basin plucked by a glacier above Woodland Lake.

straight wall across the gap it fills, the dam's relatively delicate mass would cause it to fail under the very great water pressure of the reservoir. Either the dam would shatter, or it would tip over, rotating above its base.

The arch shape, however, allows the water pressure to compress the dam against natural rock buttresses on each side. Thereby, the arch transfers the water pressure to the surrounding mountains, which will not move under any pressure for a truly unimaginable length of time.

The trail to Woodland Lake (see Hike 29) takes hikers to just a half mile from Skyscraper Reservoir. Hikers follow a trail to the next highest glacier-cut ledge on which Skyscraper hides, and the trail ends. The lowest spot in the cirque wall to the left is reached by a trackless series of ledges to the top of a tundra ridge above Bob and Betty lakes.

Full to overflowing, Skyscraper Reservoir splashes over masonry arch dam.

Skyscraper Reservoir

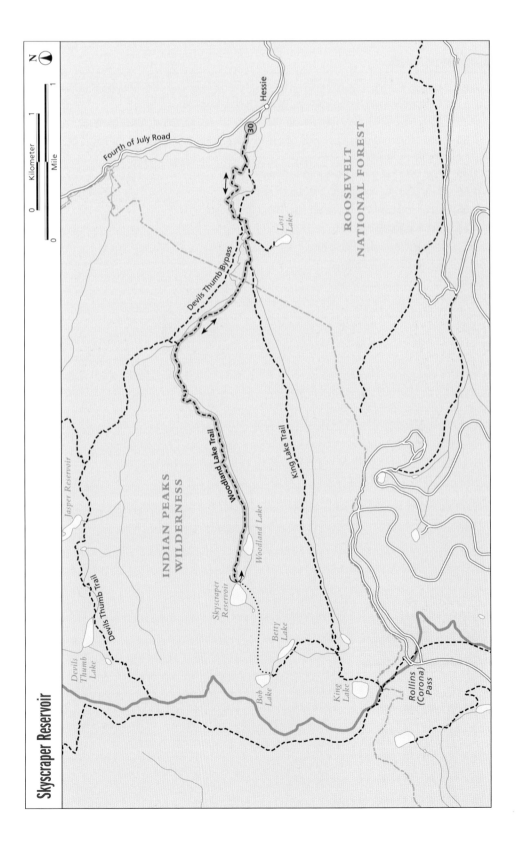

N

0   1 Kilometer

0   1 Mile

Fourth of July Road

Hessie

30

Lost Lake

ROOSEVELT NATIONAL FOREST

Devils Thumb Bypass

INDIAN PEAKS WILDERNESS

Woodland Lake Trail

King Lake Trail

Jasper Reservoir

Skyscraper Reservoir

Woodland Lake

Devils Thumb Trail

Devils Thumb Lake

Betty Lake

Bob Lake

King Lake

Rollins (Corona) Pass

Miles and Directions

0.0   Park normal passenger vehicles on south side of the road where it forks to Buckingham Campground and Hessie Trailhead. Walk to Hessie Trailhead.

0.25   If you have a high clearance vehicle, pick one of the few spaces at Hessie Trailhead.

0.85   Devils Thumb Bypass Trail heads right a few steps before a bridge. Cross the bridge on the Devils Thumb Trail.

1.35   Lost Lake Trail heads left. Continue on right fork.

1.55   King Lake Trail heads left. Continue on right fork.

2.55   Woodland Lake Trail heads left from Devils Thumb Trail.

4.55   Arrive at Woodland Lake.

5.1   Arrive at Skyscraper Reservoir.

10.2   Return to Hessie Trailhead.

10.45   Arrive back at your parked car.

31 Bob and Betty Lakes

Bob and Betty lakes are the high points in a string of lakes perched on a loop hike below the Continental Divide.

Start: Hessie Trailhead
Hiking time: About 10 hours
Distance: 12.9 miles out and back
Difficulty: Moderate
Trail surface: Dirt and rock
Best season: Summer
Other trail users: Equestrians
Canine compatibility: Dogs are permitted on handheld, 6-foot leash
Fees and permits: None for hiking. Permit is required for camping in Indian Peaks Wilderness

Trail contacts: USDA Forest Service, Boulder Ranger District, 2140 Yarmouth Ave., Boulder CO 80301; (303) 541-2500; fs.usda.gov/arp
Maps: Trails Illustrated Indian Peaks Gold Hill, USGS East Portal, Nederland
Highlights: Wildflowers, whitewater streams, Woodland Lake, Skyscraper Reservoir
Wildlife: Mule deer, elk, red squirrel, mountain chickadee
Hessie Trailhead elevation: 9,006 feet
Bob Lake elevation: 11,600 feet

Finding the trailhead: Begin at the junction of Colorado Hwy. 72 and 119 in Nederland. From the south side of Nederland, a half mile from the joining of these highways, turn right on CR 132 toward the Lake Eldora Ski Area. Where the road forks uphill (left) toward the ski area, stay on the lower (right) fork through the community of Eldora. Its pavement ends shortly. A mile past Eldora, the road forks again. Normal passenger vehicles lacking high clearance should turn around at this fork to park in locations along the south side of the road marked by signs. **GPS:** N39° 57' .1"/W105° 35' .696"

The Hessie Trailhead is a quarter mile along a road/creek bed that sometimes carries water and always is paved by cobbles hard on even booted feet. The worst parts are bordered by a trail that lifts hikers above this hassle. High clearance vehicles can make it all the way to the Hessie Trailhead and less-than-abundant parking. A bridge carries hikers across North Fork Middle Boulder Creek. Rather ironic signs near the bridge prohibit vehicles from splashing across the creek and also prohibit parking at a spot blocking an obvious vehicle ford. Across the bridge, hikers follow a distressingly rocky road used for reservoir maintenance high in Indian Peaks Wilderness.

The Hike

Bob and Betty lakes are invisible from Skyscraper Reservoir in their adjoining cirque to the south. But, a reasonably easy ascent (no trail) over the lowest part of the cirque wall leads to a marvelous (aside from the mosquitoes at Bob and Betty) circle hike. Follow the trail to Woodland Lake and Skyscraper Reservoir (Hikes 29 and 30). Cross the outlet stream below the Skyscraper Reservoir dam. Pick what appears to be the least steep ascent to the low point in the cirque wall above Skyscraper (11,760 feet),

Betty Lake decorates tree line below the Continental Divide.

Bob and Betty lakes sit below the Continental Divide, not as seen from ridge above Skyscraper Reservoir.

Bob and Betty Lakes

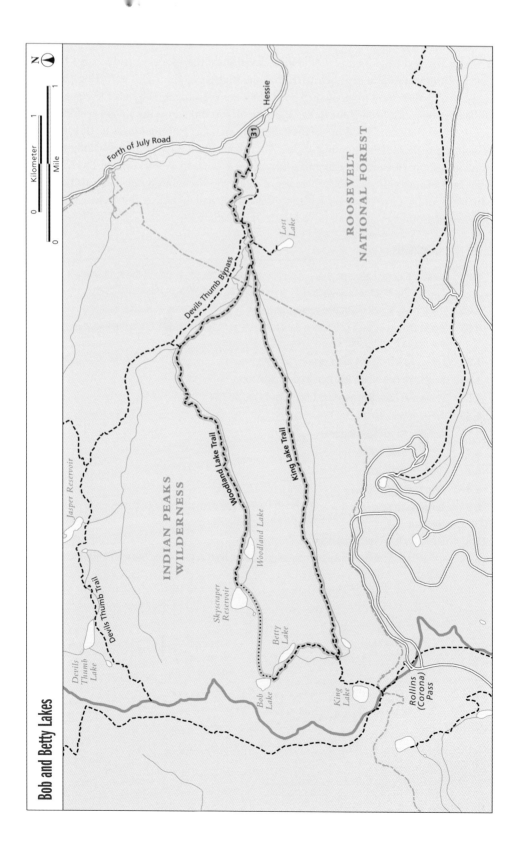

Forth of July Road

31

Hessie

ROOSEVELT
NATIONAL FOREST

Lost
Lake

Devils Thumb Bypass

Jasper Reservoir

INDIAN PEAKS
WILDERNESS

Woodland Lake Trail

King Lake Trail

Skyscraper
Reservoir

Woodland Lake

Devils Thumb Trail

Devils
Thumb
Lake

Betty
Lake

Bob
Lake

King
Lake

Rollins
(Corona)
Pass

Kilometer

Mile

a tundra-covered ridge that is the highest elevation of the loop. From the ridge top, Bob and Betty are fairly near below (Bob is the highest, to the right) and King Lake is obvious further away in its own cirque below the Continental Divide. Descend by the least steep route, headed for Betty (less difficult terrain). Cross the stream connecting Bob and Betty and head upstream (right) on the faint path that leads to Bob, out of sight from Betty behind a small ridge. After that visit, retrace your steps along the southwest shore of Betty to descend to the King Lake Trail. A left turn on the King Lake Trail among willows and spruces drops steeply to the whitewater of South Fork Middle Boulder Creek. Thereafter, the grade is unchallenging to the Indian Peaks Wilderness Boundary and on out to Hessie Trailhead.

Miles and Directions

0.0   West of Eldora, park a normal passenger vehicle on the south side of the road where it forks to Buckingham Campground and Hessie Trailhead. Walk to Hessie Trailhead.

0.25   If you have a high clearance vehicle, pick one of the few spaces at Hessie Trailhead.

0.85   Devils Thumb Bypass Trail heads right a few steps before a bridge. Cross the bridge on the Devils Thumb Trail.

1.35   Lost Lake Trail heads left. Continue on right fork.

1.55   King Lake Trail heads left. Continue on right fork.

2.55   Woodland Lake Trail heads left from Devils Thumb Trail.

4.55   Arrive at Woodland Lake.

5.1   Arrive at Skyscraper Reservoir.

5.9   Arrive at Betty Lake.

6.1   Arrive at Bob Lake.

6.3   Return to Betty Lake.

6.8   Descend to King Lake Trail and turn left (unless you want to detour 0.4 miles up to King Lake).

11.8   Arrive back at Hessie Trailhead.

12.05   Arrive back at normal clearance passenger car parked at the fork in the road west of Eldora.

32 King Lake

King Lake should be part of a loop past Woodland Lake, Skyscraper Reservoir, and Betty and Bob lakes. It is only a 0.8-mile detour after Betty Lake, and the lush tundra bordering the lake leading to a large perpetual snowbank between the Continental Divide and the lake's western shore is worth the extra distance.

Start: Hessie Trailhead or Rollins Pass

Hiking time: About 10 hours

Distance: 13.7 out and back or 6.4 one-way downhill

Difficulty: Moderate

Trail surface: Dirt and rock

Best season: Summer

Other trail users: Equestrians

Canine compatibility: Dogs are permitted on handheld, 6-foot leash

Fees and permits: None for hiking. Permit is required for camping in Indian Peaks Wilderness

Trail contacts: USDA Forest Service, Boulder Ranger District, 2140 Yarmouth Ave., Boulder

CO 80301; (303) 541-2500; fs.usda.gov/arp or USDA Forest Service, Sulphur Ranger District, PO Box 10, 9 Ten Mile Dr., Granby CO 80446; (970-887-4100); fs.usda.gov/arp

Maps: Trails Illustrated Indian Peaks Gold Hill, USGS East Portal, Nederland

Highlights: Wildflowers, whitewater streams, Woodland Lake, Skyscraper Reservoir, Bob and Betty lakes

Wildlife: Mule deer, elk, red squirrel, mountain chickadee

Hessie Trailhead elevation: 9,006 feet

King Lake elevation: 11,431 feet

High point via Bob and Betty lakes: 11,760 feet

Finding the trailhead: For Hessie Trailhead, begin at the junction of Colorado Hwy. 72 and 119 in Nederland. From the south side of Nederland, a half mile from the joining of these highways, turn right on CR 132 toward the Lake Eldora Ski Area. Where the road forks uphill (left) toward the ski area, stay on the lower (right) fork through the community of Eldora. Its pavement ends shortly. A mile past Eldora, the road forks again. Normal passenger vehicles lacking high clearance should turn around at this fork to park in locations along the south side of the road marked by signs. **GPS:** N39° 57' .1"/W105° 35' .696"

The Hessie Trailhead is a quarter mile along a road/creek bed that sometimes carries water and always is paved by cobbles hard on even booted feet. The worst parts are bordered by a trail that lifts hikers above this hassle. High clearance vehicles can make it all the way to the Hessie Trailhead and less-than-abundant parking. A bridge carries hikers across North Fork Middle Boulder Creek. Rather ironic signs near the bridge prohibit vehicles from splashing across the creek and also prohibit parking at a spot blocking an obvious vehicle ford. Across the bridge, hikers follow a distressingly rocky road used for reservoir maintenance high in Indian Peaks Wilderness.

Finding the trailhead: For Rollins Pass Trailhead (also called Corona Pass), start on the West Slope opposite Winter Park Ski Area along US Hwy. 40. Ascent of the 14-mile rough road to the pass takes about an hour of historic scenery. The road ends at the pass (11,671 feet). GPS: N39° 56' .07"/W105° 40' .55"

The Hike

King Lake is a worthwhile detour on the glorious loop hike that begins and ends at Hessie Trailhead (see Hike 31).

However, far the easiest way to reach King Lake is from Rollins Pass. Hikers can leave the pass, surmounting a small hill, to walk down an easy tundra slope, covered with brilliant floral jewels in July, and drop on a trail through a gap between cliffs along the Continental Divide along a simple trail to King Lake obvious in its cirque below. Of course, the trudge back up to a car left in Rollins Pass is less pleasant. Hence, the lure is very strong for hikers to continue a downhill hike, passing through various life zones along whitewater streams to Hessie Trailhead.

With grades that generally are not knee crunching, it is an ideal downhill hike. At least it is ideal for everyone except the saintly driver who is willing to drop hikers at Rollins Pass to descend to Hessie while their extremely good friend drives to meet them. The chauffeur has to drive 14 miles down the unpaved road (admittedly, the

King Lake perches in glacier-carved basin below the Continental Divide.

Paintbrush wildflowers color the edge of King Lake.

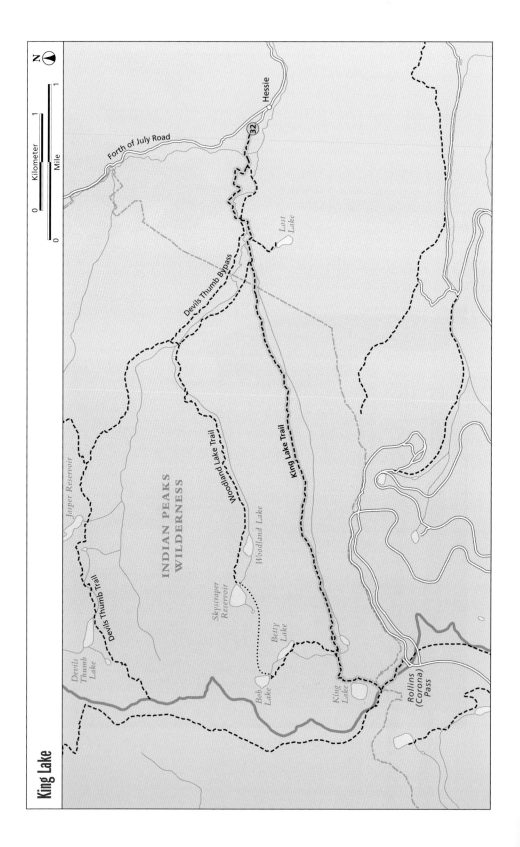

King Lake

N

0   Kilometer   1

0   Mile   1

Forth of July Road

Hessie

32

Devils Thumb Bypass

Lost Lake

Jasper Reservoir

Devils Thumb Trail

Devils Thumb Lake

INDIAN PEAKS WILDERNESS

Woodland Lake Trail

Skyscraper Reservoir

Woodland Lake

King Lake Trail

Bob Lake

Betty Lake

King Lake

Rollins (Corona) Pass

scenery is very exciting) to Winter Park Ski Area. Then a left turn leads up tortuous curves to Berthoud Pass and down to turn east on Interstate Hwy. 70 as far as an exit for Central City. Here, a very pleasant road succeeds in its designed purpose of luring interstate motorists into Central City's countless casinos.

The Colorado legislature legalized gambling in Central City for its supposedly historic role in the 1860s mining town. The legislature thus displayed an unsurprisingly vague knowledge of their state's history. In truth, the founding fathers of Central City outlawed gambling dens, brothels, and lawyers.

Thus, unaided by true history, the saintly chauffer must wind through a tortuous tangle of steep streets laid out for horse-drawn vehicles. The driver on reaching the bottom of Clear Creek Canyon turns left in the adjacent community of Blackhawk, where air is infinitely cleaner (though less historic) than when its smelters for Central City ore belched out pollution reminiscent of the surface of the planet Venus. The driver reaches Hessie Trailhead (GPS: N39° 59' .714"/W105° 38' .052") still hours before his extremely good friends arrive from a day far more exciting than any day available in Central City, I suppose. Perhaps the driver can enliven the wait with a walk up to Lost Lake (Hike 33) or even climb the Devils Thumb Trail to share part of the hike from King Lake with very good friends. The driver must not, however, accidentally walk past the King Lake Trail in a meadow 1.55 miles from Hessie Trailhead, and thereby miss a rendezvous with his very good friends, causing a king-sized mess.

Miles and Directions

0.0   From Rollins Pass, stroll along the High Lonesome Trail across alpine tundra on the Continental Divide.

0.3   Turn right to descend a trail that avoids cliffs on either side. Do not slide down a snow bank into King Lake.

1.0   Arrive at King Lake to enjoy yet more tundra flowers.

6.4   Arrive at Hessie Trailhead.

33 Lost Lake

Start: Hessie Trailhead
Hiking time: About 3 hours
Distance: 3 miles out and back
Difficulty: Easy
Trail surface: Dirt and rock
Best season: Summer and fall (fall color in aspen and mountain maple)
Other trail users: Equestrians
Canine compatibility: Dogs are permitted on handheld, 6-foot leash
Fees and permits: None

Trail contacts: USDA Forest Service, Boulder Ranger District, 2140 Yarmouth Ave., Boulder CO 80301; (303) 541-2500; fs.usda.gov/arp
Maps: Trails Illustrated Indian Peaks Gold Hill, USGS Nederland
Highlights: Wildflowers, whitewater streams, old mines, Lost Lake
Wildlife: Mule deer, elk, red squirrel, mountain chickadee
Hessie Trailhead elevation: 9,006 feet
Lost Lake Elevation: 9,800 feet

Finding the trailhead: Begin at the junction of Colorado Hwy. 72 and 119 in Nederland. From the south side of Nederland, a half mile from the joining of these highways, turn right on CR 132 toward the Lake Eldora Ski Area. Where the road forks uphill (left) toward the ski area, stay on the lower (right) fork through the community of Eldora. Its pavement ends shortly. A mile past Eldora, the road forks again. Normal passenger vehicles lacking high clearance should turn around at this fork to park in locations along the south side of the road marked by signs. **GPS:** N39° 57' .1"/W105° 35' .696"

The Hessie Trailhead is a quarter mile along a road/creek bed that sometimes carries water and always is paved by cobbles hard on even booted feet. The worst parts are bordered by a trail that lifts hikers above this hassle. High clearance vehicles can make it all the way to the Hessie Trailhead and less-than-abundant parking. A bridge carries hikers across North Fork Middle Boulder Creek. Rather ironic signs near the bridge prohibit vehicles from splashing across the creek and also prohibit parking at a spot blocking an obvious vehicle ford. Across the bridge, hikers follow a distressingly rocky road used for reservoir maintenance high in Indian Peaks Wilderness. **GPS:** N39° 59' .714"/W105° 38' .052"

The Hike

It is puzzling that so many lakes carry the name "Lost." (There is another, for instance, at the end of Lost Lake Trail a short way north in Rocky Mountain National Park.) How does a lake get lost? It is in the same place today as it was yesterday. Admittedly, lakes are geologically ephemeral features. But, they require millennia to fill with dirt and disappear. Perhaps lakes are lost due to lack of trail guide authors. Or maybe namers of the lakes admire alliteration, which seems poetic, like most lakes.

Lost Lake is too popular to be lost. The cobbled road from the parking area to Hessie Trailhead is rough and sometimes flooded, but a real path alongside lifts hikers above the worst parts. A bridge carries hikers across North Fork Middle Boulder Creek to a stony Devils Thumb Trail leading to another bridge about 0.6 mile further at the intersection of the Devils Thumb Trail and the Devils Thumb Bypass. Pass by the bypass and cross the bridge over South Fork Middle Boulder Creek to continue on the Devils Thumb Trail. From simple lulling pleasantness within deep forest, the creek volume rises to thunder as it rushes through a rock chute in a waterfall unnamed on maps but called Hessie Falls by some locals.

After a half mile from the bridge, the Lost Lake Trail bears left from the Devils Thumb Trail. Along the half-mile stretch to Lost Lake, hikers encounter signs of the area's mining history. Three kettle-like holes on the left side of the trail (two together followed by one more) mark where a lot of labor was expended without hitting pay dirt.

From Lost Lake itself, however, it is easy to see a collapsed mining structure and tailings further east, hanging on the slope south of the lake. These efforts made Hessie a supply center in a three-year boom after 1890. The town was founded by Captain J. H. Davis and named for his wife. The multitude of mining claims that surround the lake on the map as far as the Indian Peaks Wilderness boundary to the west likely are played out but may explain why Lost Lake was lost to Indian Peaks Wilderness. An open view from the east shore extends to ragged Continental Divide peaks within the wilderness.

Lost Lake is particularly colorful with quaking aspen leaves in fall because aspen pioneered ground cleared by mining in the 1890s.

South Fork Middle Boulder Creek crashes over Hessie Falls.

Lost Lake reflects Indian Peaks from just outside wilderness boundary.

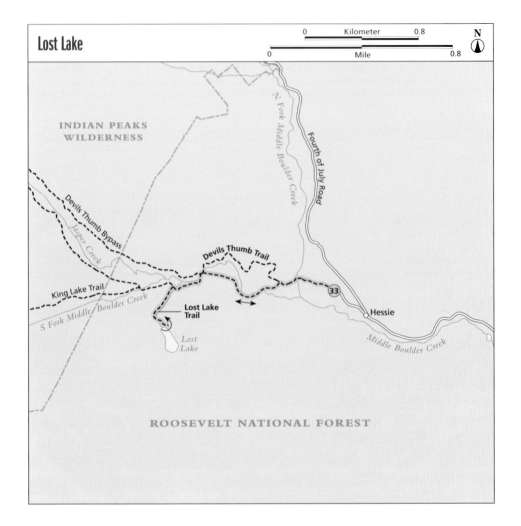

Miles and Directions

0.0   Park normal passenger cars at fork in road west of Eldora. Walk west on left fork along a cobbled road often filled with water or on a parallel path to the right above parts of the road.

0.25   Reach Hessie Trailhead and cross a bridge over North Fork Middle Boulder Creek to ascend rocky road of Devils Thumb Trail.

0.85   Reach another bridge and cross over South Fork Middle Boulder Creek.

1.35   Bear left on the Lost Lake Trail from the Devils Thumb Trail.

1.85   Arrive at Lost Lake.

3.7   Arrive back at fork in road parking.

West of the Continental Divide

Upper Lake remains surrounded by snow in August.

34 Watanga Lake

The hike to Watanga Lake switches from steep to relatively gentle grades in a stair-step pattern cut by glaciers.

Start: Roaring Fork Trailhead
Hiking time: About 7 hours
Distance: 8.5 miles out and back
Difficulty: Difficult
Trail surface: Dirt
Best season: Summer
Other trail users: Equestrians
Canine compatibility: Dogs are permitted on handheld, 6-foot leashes
Fees and permits: A parking fee or interagency recreational area pass required. Permit is required for camping

Trail contacts: USDA Forest Service, Sulphur Ranger District, PO Box 10, 9 Ten Mile Dr., Granby CO 80446; (970) 877-4100, fs.usda.gov/arp
Maps: Trails Illustrated Indian Peaks Gold Hill; USGS Shadow Mountain, Isolation Peak
Highlights: Valley of Roaring Fork, Watanga Lake
Wildlife: Mule deer, elk, moose, red squirrel, mountain chickadee
Roaring Fork Trailhead elevation: 8,281 feet
Watanga Lake elevation: 10,790 feet

Finding the trailhead: From the north side of the town of Granby at the intersection of US Hwy. 40 and 34, drive north 5.4 miles and turn east onto Arapaho Bay Road. The turn to Arapaho Bay is about 11 miles south of Grand Lake on Hwy. 34. Drive 8.8 miles along the south shore of Lake Granby and turn left for 0.8 miles to Roaring Fork Trailhead. **GPS:** N40° 07'/W105° 40' .55"

The Hike

Watanga was an Arapaho prominent in his tribe at the end of the nineteenth century. He took part in the brutal self-torture of the sun dance, signed an 1890 treaty with the Euro-Americans, and served as a captain of Indian police. He was also a delegate for his tribe to Washington, and deputy sheriff in the generation following the Plains Indian wars.

In Arapaho, Watanga means Black Coyote, but hikers more likely will remember the lake for its abundant trout population. From Roaring Fork Trailhead at Arapaho Bay on Lake Granby, the trail traverses lodgepole pine forests much battered by pine beetles and interspersed by open marshes. (Roaring Fork is not named for a noisy eating utensil, but for a whitewater stream along what was a fork of Arapaho Creek before the damming of Lake Granby turned Arapaho Creek into Arapaho Bay.) Beyond a broad, shrubby meadow where the trail crosses Roaring Fork, the Watanga Lake Trail branches left, and the gentle grade ends. Switchbacks lessen the work, and views down to the Fraser Valley and up to the Continental Divide provide valid reasons to pause. The trail passes through flower-filled subalpine forest until passing over a terminal moraine that impounds Watanga Lake.

Watanga Lake is home to abundant trout.

Miles and Directions

0.0   Begin the hike at Roaring Fork Trailhead.

0.I   Limber your legs for a steep ascent.

0.5   Rest to look over Lake Granby.

1.0   Cross a bridge over Roaring Fork.

2.5   Cross Roaring Fork to meet a trail fork where the trail to Mount Irving Hale goes right and Watanga Lake Trail heads left to encounter a steep climb.

4.25 Arrive at Watanga Lake and watch the trout jump.

8.5   Arrive back at the Roaring Fork Trailhead.

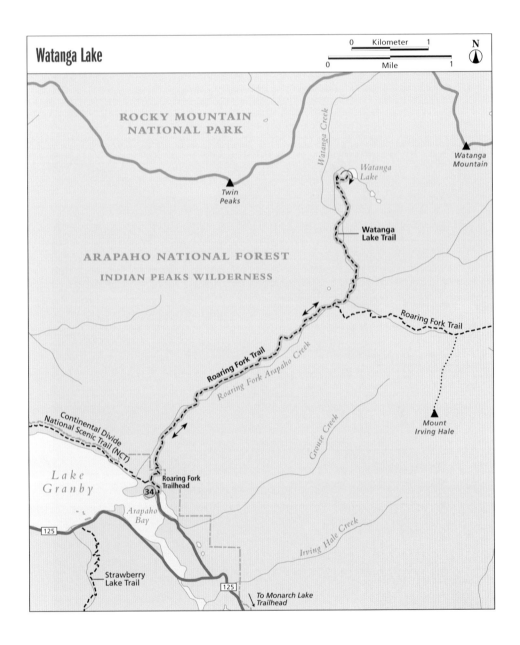

Watanga Lake

ROCKY MOUNTAIN
NATIONAL PARK

Watanga Creek

Twin
Peaks

*Watanga
Lake*

▲ Watanga
Mountain

**Watanga
Lake Trail**

ARAPAHO NATIONAL FOREST

INDIAN PEAKS WILDERNESS

Roaring Fork Trail

Roaring Fork Trail

Roaring Fork Arapaho Creek

Grouse Creek

▲ Mount
Irving Hale

Continental Divide
National Scenic Trail (NCT)

*Lake
Granby*

Roaring Fork
Trailhead

34

*Arapaho
Bay*

125

Strawberry
Lake Trail

125

Irving Hale Creek

To Monarch Lake
Trailhead

0   Kilometer   1

0   Mile   1

N

Black Coyote is the meaning of the Arapaho word Watanga. *Hikers might see buffy coyotes at this lake but no black coyotes.*

35 Irving Hale Divide

The Irving Hale Divide hike passes from the trail branching to Watanga Lake (Hike34) over the ridge between Roaring Fork and Hell Canyon.

Start: Roaring Fork Trailhead
Hiking time: About 7 hours
Distance: 8.2 miles out and back
Difficulty: Difficult
Trail surface: Dirt
Best season: Summer
Other trail users: Equestrians
Canine compatibility: Dogs are permitted on handheld, 6-foot leashes
Fees and permits: A parking fee or interagency recreational area pass. Permit is required for camping

Trail contacts: USDA Forest Service, Sulphur Ranger District, PO Box 10, 9 Ten Mile Dr., Granby CO 80446; (970) 877-4100, fs.usda. gov/arp
Maps: Trails Illustrated Indian Peaks Gold Hill; USGS Shadow Mountain, Isolation Peak
Highlights: Valley of Roaring Fork, wildflowers, Irving Hale Divide
Wildlife: Mule deer, elk, moose, red squirrel, mountain chickadee
Roaring Fork Trailhead elevation: 8,281 feet
Irving Hale Divide elevation: 11,195 feet

Finding the trailhead: From the north side of the town of Granby at the intersection of US Hwy. 40 and 34, drive north 5.4 miles and turn east onto Arapaho Bay Road. The turn to Arapaho Bay is about 11 miles south of Grand Lake on Hwy. 34. Drive 8.8 miles along the south shore of Lake Granby and turn left for 0.8 miles to Roaring Fork Trailhead. **GPS:** N40° .07"/W105° 40' .55"

The Hike

Whatever the references to Hell on the initial climb from the trailhead or while puffing and panting up the right fork from the Watanga Lake Trail split in the valley containing Roaring Fork, colorful wildflower species far exceed infernal puns as hikers gasp to the broad saddle below Mount Irving Hale. Once on the Divide, the trail descends slightly through fields of glacier lilies fed by deep snow banks melting in June. A fine view of the Continental Divide to the east rises above the flowers. At the top of Irving Hale Divide, satisfied hikers rejoice in the floral wonder and retrace the steep slope down the Roaring Fork Trail back to their cars, which is easier than descending into Hell Canyon.

Miles and Directions

0.0	Begin the hike at Roaring Fork Trailhead.
0.l	Limber your legs for a steep ascent.
0.5	Stop to look over Lake Granby.
1.0	Cross a bridge over Roaring Fork.

Broad open spaces atop Irving Hale Divide offer grand views of peaks surrounding Hell Canyon.

2.5   Cross Roaring Fork to meet a trail fork where the trail to Mount Irving Hale goes right and Watanga Lake Trail heads left. Head right across a deceptively level meadow.

3.0   Begin lung-popping climb up north-facing canyon wall.

3.4   Be thankful for moderating grade.

4.1   Enjoy wildflowers at Irving Hale Divide.

8.2   Retrace your route from the top of Irving Hale Divide to Roaring Fork Trailhead.

Irving Hale Divide

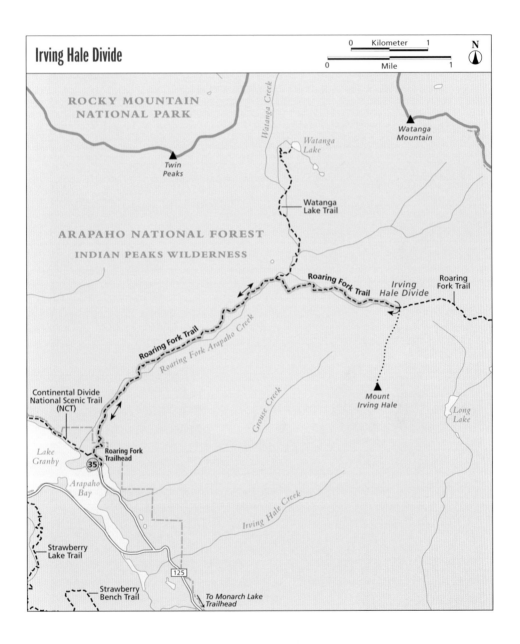

0   Kilometer   1

0   Mile   1

N

ROCKY MOUNTAIN
NATIONAL PARK

Watanga Creek

Watanga
Mountain

Twin
Peaks

Watanga
Lake

ARAPAHO NATIONAL FOREST

INDIAN PEAKS WILDERNESS

Watanga
Lake Trail

Roaring Fork Trail

Irving
Hale Divide

Roaring
Fork Trail

Roaring Fork Trail

Roaring Fork Trail

Roaring Fork Arapaho Creek

Grouse Creek

Mount
Irving Hale

Long
Lake

Continental Divide
National Scenic Trail
(NCT)

Lake
Granby

Roaring Fork
Trailhead

35

Arapaho
Bay

Strawberry
Lake Trail

Irving Hale Creek

125

Strawberry
Bench Trail

To Monarch Lake
Trailhead

Abundant wildflowers enrich the steep trail up Irving Hale Divide.

36 Mount Irving Hale

Mount Irving Hale is not as high as most mountains in this guide; it is however, fortuitously located for superb views.

Start: Roaring Fork Trailhead
Hiking time: About 8 hours
Distance: 11.5 miles out and back
Difficulty: Difficult
Trail surface: Dirt
Best season: Summer
Other trail users: Equestrians
Canine compatibility: Dogs are permitted on handheld, 6-foot leashes
Fees and permits: A parking fee or interagency recreational area pass. Permit is required for camping

Trail contacts: USDA Forest Service, Sulphur Ranger District, PO Box 10, 9 Ten Mile Dr., Granby CO 80446; (970) 877-4100, fs.usda. gov/arp
Maps: Trails Illustrated Indian Peaks Gold Hill; USGS Shadow Mountain, Isolation Peak
Highlights: Valley of Roaring Fork, wildflowers, Irving Hale Divide, Mount Irving Hale
Wildlife: Mule deer, elk, moose, red squirrel, mountain chickadee
Roaring Fork Trailhead elevation: 8,281 feet
Mount Irving Hale elevation: 11,754 feet

Finding the trailhead: From the north side of the town of Granby at the intersection of US Hwy. 40 and 34, drive north 5.4 miles and turn east onto Arapaho Bay Road. The turn to Arapaho Bay is about 11 miles south of Grand Lake on Hwy. 34. Drive 8.8 miles along the south shore of Lake Granby and turn left for 0.8 miles to Roaring Fork Trailhead. **GPS:** N40° .07"/W105° 40' .55"

The Hike

From the Irving Hale Divide (see Hike 35), Mount Irving Hale is an easy ascent south on a pathless tundra ridge avoiding a cliffy drop to Hell Canyon. Two large piles of rock (cairns) are visible atop the double summit of Irving Hale that from below resemble two climbers looking over the canyon. Blocking boulders precede a false summit. The true top is not large, but the views repay all effort getting there. Huge Lake Granby extends through Middle Park toward the Gore Range defining the western horizon. The ragged spine of Indian Peaks, accented by Mount Toll and Paiute Peak, rises on the southeast. Crawford and Long lakes are far below your boots beneath cliffs on Irving Hale.

The view from Mount Irving Hale indicates its lucky location for enjoying higher peaks around Hell Canyon.

Miles and Directions

0.0   Begin the hike at Roaring Fork Trailhead.

0.I   Limber your legs for a steep ascent.

0.5   Stop to look over Lake Granby.

1.0   Cross a bridge over Roaring Fork.

2.5   Cross Roaring Fork to meet a trail fork where the trail to Mount Irving Hale goes right and Watanga Lake Trail heads left. Head right across a deceptively level meadow.

3.0   Begin lung-popping climb up north-facing canyon wall.

3.4   Be thankful for moderating grade.

4.1   Enjoy wildflowers at Irving Hale Divide. Turn right to imagine best route up the double summit of Mount Irving Hale.

5.75   Reach the top of Mount Irving Hale.

11.5   Arrive back at the Roaring Fork Trailhead.

Mount Irving Hale

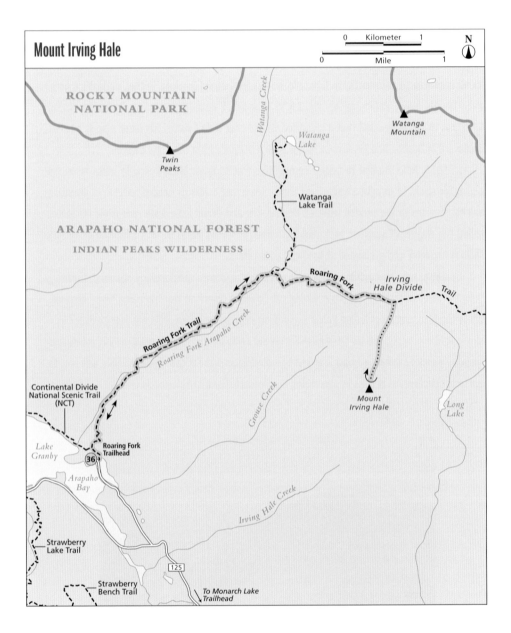

Kilometer 0 — 1
Mile 0 — 1

N

ROCKY MOUNTAIN
NATIONAL PARK

Watanga Creek

Watanga Mountain

Twin Peaks

Watanga Lake

Watanga Lake Trail

ARAPAHO NATIONAL FOREST

INDIAN PEAKS WILDERNESS

Roaring Fork

Irving Hale Divide Trail

Roaring Fork Trail

Roaring Fork Arapaho Creek

Grouse Creek

Mount Irving Hale

Long Lake

Continental Divide National Scenic Trail (NCT)

Lake Granby

Roaring Fork Trailhead

36

Arapaho Bay

Irving Hale Creek

Strawberry Lake Trail

Strawberry Bench Trail

125

To Monarch Lake Trailhead

GENERAL IRVING HALE

Irving Hale was so noteworthy in Colorado history that even Ellsworth Bethel, normally a complete fanatic about defending his wonderful scheme of naming the Indian Peaks for Native American tribes, suggested that a mountain should bear Hale's name. His name also is on Hale Boulevard in Denver, and his bronze image is on a plaque within the state capitol.

In 1878, Hale studied to take a competitive test to enter West Point. To make time and money for study, he bought a wagon and a mule team that evidently needed only slight direction and began a freighting service between Central City and Grand Lake. Hale read while his mules pulled the wagon all summer back and forth over Berthoud Pass. He was admitted to the US Military Academy and graduated at the head of his class.

By 1898, Hale had achieved the rank of general and was spectacularly successful leading Colorado soldiers in the Philippines during the Spanish–American War. He came home honored, but by the time namers of Indian Peaks began their naming campaign, Hale was incapacitated by a stroke. At their urging, the US Geological Survey set aside the rule that banned naming mountains for living people. Exhibiting spunk admired by mountaineers, the vocally impaired Hale was able to add to the endless list of puns by expressing his pleasure that his peak was so close to Hell Canyon.

The view from the top of Mount Irving Hale drops into Hell Canyon.

37 Stone Lake

Although this name could be justly applied to most lakes in this guide, the rounded boulders around the lake testify to the appropriateness of its label.

Start: Roaring Fork Trailhead
Hiking time: About 12 hours
Distance: 13.5 miles loop
Difficulty: Difficult
Trail surface: Dirt
Best season: Summer
Other trail users: Equestrians
Canine compatibility: Dogs are permitted on handheld, 6-foot leashes
Fees and permits: A parking fee or interagency recreational area pass. Permit is required for camping

Trail contacts: USDA Forest Service, Sulphur Ranger District, PO Box 10, 9 Ten Mile Dr., Granby CO 80446; (970) 877-4100, fs.usda.gov/arp
Maps: Trails Illustrated Indian Peaks Gold Hill; USGS Shadow Mountain, Isolation Peak
Highlights: Valley of Roaring Fork, wildflowers, Irving Hale Divide, Hell Canyon, Stone Lake
Wildlife: Mule deer, elk, moose, red squirrel, mountain chickadee
Roaring Fork Trailhead elevation: 8,281 feet
Irving Hale Divide elevation: 11,195 feet
Stone Lake elevation: 10,643 feet

Finding the trailhead: From the north side of the town of Granby at the intersection of US Hwy. 40 and 34, drive north 5.4 miles and turn east onto Arapaho Bay Road. The turn to Arapaho Bay is about 11 miles south of Grand Lake on Hwy. 34. Drive 8.8 miles along the south shore of Lake Granby and turn left for 0.8 miles to Roaring Fork Trailhead. GPS: N40° .07"/W105° 40' .55" The hike leads to Monarch Lake Trailhead, 2 miles south. **GPS:** N40° 06'/W105° 44' .48'"

The Hike

From the Irving Hale Divide (see Hike 35), the trail descends past a pond, flowery meadows, and Marten Peak views to meet Hell Canyon at its higher reaches, below the Continental Divide. Hikers reach the canyon floor at the outlet stream from Stone Lake. Cliffs to the left and stream to the right assisted by cairns where the trail grows faint direct hikers to the lake's shore a couple of miles from Irving Hale Divide.

There are a notable number of boulders around Stone Lake. But the name appropriately applies to almost any lake in this book. Stone Lake lies in a stone basin glaciers scoured, using stones carried like an icy rasp. Stone Lake is less deep than many lakes created by glaciers in an identical fashion. The impressive rounded stones along its shore are interspersed by little meadows and trees of the forest's upper edge.

On the way to the lake down the very steep south-facing wall of Hell Canyon, the thought of heading back up this grade encourages some hikers to continue descending by following the outlet from Stone Lake along the occasionally marshy canyon floor down to Crawford Lake. An indistinct path incites further descent to Long Lake, which commits hikers to pushing all the way down the canyon to the Cascade Creek Trail for a right turn and loop return to Roaring Fork Trailhead via a two-mile jaunt along the road from Monarch Lake Trailhead.

Boulders along its shore gave Stone Lake its name.

Miles and Directions

0.0   Begin the hike at Roaring Fork Trailhead.

0.I   Limber your legs for a steep ascent.

0.5   Stop to look over Lake Granby.

1.0   Cross a bridge over Roaring Fork.

2.5   Cross Roaring Fork to meet a trail fork where the trail to Mount Irving Hale goes right and Watanga Lake Trail heads left. Head right across a deceptively level meadow.

3.0   Begin lung-popping climb up north-facing canyon wall.

3.4   Be thankful for moderating grade.

4.1   Enjoy wildflowers at Irving Hale Divide.

4.75 Begin a steep descent along trail into Hell Canyon.

5.85 Trail reaches the canyon floor.

6.15 Arrive at Stone Lake. Descend along the outlet stream.

7.45 Arrive at Crawford Lake.

7.85 Arrive at Long Lake.

9.65 Stumble onto Cascade Creek Trail. Turn right.

10.3 Reach the junction of Cascade Creek and Buchanan Pass trails. Bear right toward Monarch Lake.

11.15 Leave Indian Peaks Wilderness at Monarch Lake.

11.90 Arrive at Monarch Lake Trailhead. Walk along the road toward Roaring Fork Trailhead.

13.90 Arrive back at the Roaring Fork Trailhead.

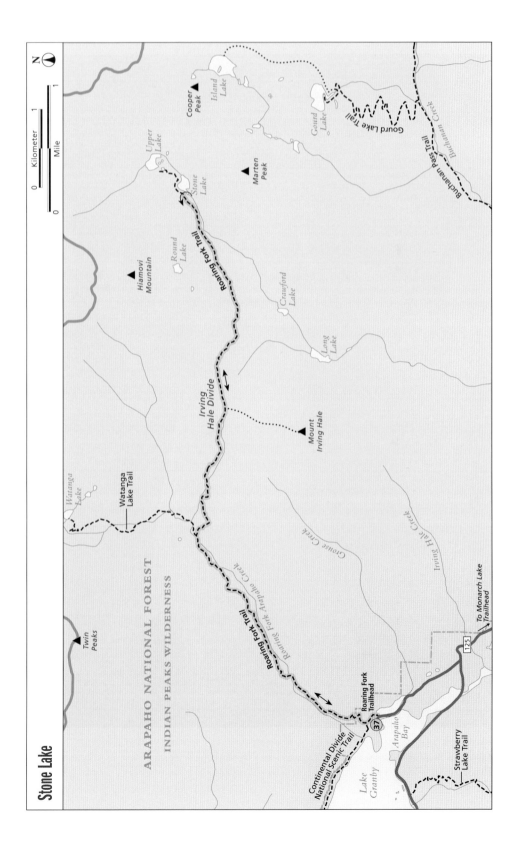

Stone Lake

Hiamovi is a Cheyenne name used on a peak dominating the upper end of Hell Canyon. Likely the name was familiar to the Cheyenne girl who played with this doll from the Eagle Plume collection along Colorado Highway 7 near Allenspark.

38 Upper Lake

The basin containing Upper Lake looks like the glacier that carved it melted yesterday.

Start: Roaring Fork Trailhead
Hiking time: About 13 hours
Distance: 15.5 miles loop
Difficulty: Difficult
Trail surface: Dirt
Best season: Summer
Other trail users: Equestrians
Canine compatibility: Dogs are permitted on handheld, 6-foot leashes
Fees and permits: A parking fee or interagency recreational area pass. Camping permit is required
Trail contacts: USDA Forest Service, Sulphur Ranger District, PO Box 10, 9 Ten Mile Dr.,
Granby CO 80446; (970) 877-4100, fs.usda.gov/arp
Maps: Trails Illustrated Indian Peaks Gold Hill; USGS Shadow Mountain, Isolation Peak
Highlights: Valley of Roaring Fork, wildflowers, Irving Hale Divide, Hell Canyon, Stone Lake, Upper Lake
Wildlife: Mule deer, elk, moose, red squirrel, mountain chickadee
Roaring Fork Trailhead elevation: 8,281 feet
Irving Hale Divide elevation: 11,195 feet
Upper Lake elevation: 10,730 feet

Finding the trailhead: From the north side of the town of Granby at the intersection of US Hwy. 40 and 34, drive north 5.4 miles and turn east onto Arapaho Bay Road. The turn to Arapaho Bay is about 11 miles south of Grand Lake on Hwy. 34. Drive 8.8 miles along the south shore of Lake Granby and turn left for 0.8 miles to Roaring Fork Trailhead. **GPS:** N40° 07'/W105° 40' .55"

The Hike

After circling the north shore of Stone Lake (see Hike 37), the Roaring Fork Trail climbs a short way to end at a minor pond very close to Upper Lake. Above, rising in a dizzyingly huge bowl of the Continental Divide, the scene in August looks as though the most recent glacier melted yesterday. From a geologic perspective, it did. Beyond the lake, there is no trail but also no barriers to following a stream along the steep flank of Hiamovi Mountain to a broad tundra meadow. A final steep walk to a less high point on the Divide, leads from Hell Canyon to a pass overlooking Paradise Park in Rocky Mountain National Park. The pass is some 810 feet higher than Upper Lake. Theoretically, hikers here stand on the boundary between Paradise and Hell, but the view in all directions is heavenly. (See photo on page 170.)

Two sources (though one might be copying the other) cite the name Hiamovi as meaning "High Chief." For Euro-Americans who attached Indian names to Indian Peaks while unavoidably preserving their own cultural orientation, "High Chief" might be a synonym for God, which another source states. For Indian Peaks namers, having God Mountain oversee Paradise Park and Hell Canyon might have had understandable appeal. On the other hand, a Cheyenne named Hiamovi helped illustrate and provide text for a book called *The Indians' Book* in 1908.

Upper Lake sits in a predictably snowy environment at tree line.

Miles and Directions

0.0 Begin the hike at Roaring Fork Trailhead.

0.1 Limber your legs for a steep ascent.

0.5 Stop to look over Lake Granby.

1.0 Cross a bridge over Roaring Fork.

2.5 Cross Roaring Fork to meet a trail fork where the trail to Mount Irving Hale goes right and Watanga Lake Trail heads left. Head right across a deceptively level meadow.

3.0 Begin lung-popping climb up north-facing canyon wall.

3.4 Be thankful for moderating grade.

4.1 Enjoy wildflowers at Irving Hale Divide.

4.75 Begin a steep descent along trail into Hell Canyon.

5.85 Trail reaches canyon floor.

6.15 Arrive at Stone Lake. Ascend along inlet stream.

6.65 Arrive at Upper Lake.

7.65 Arrive at pass overlooking Paradise Park in Rocky Mountain National Park. Return to Stone Lake.

9.15 Arrive back at Stone Lake. Descend along the outlet stream.

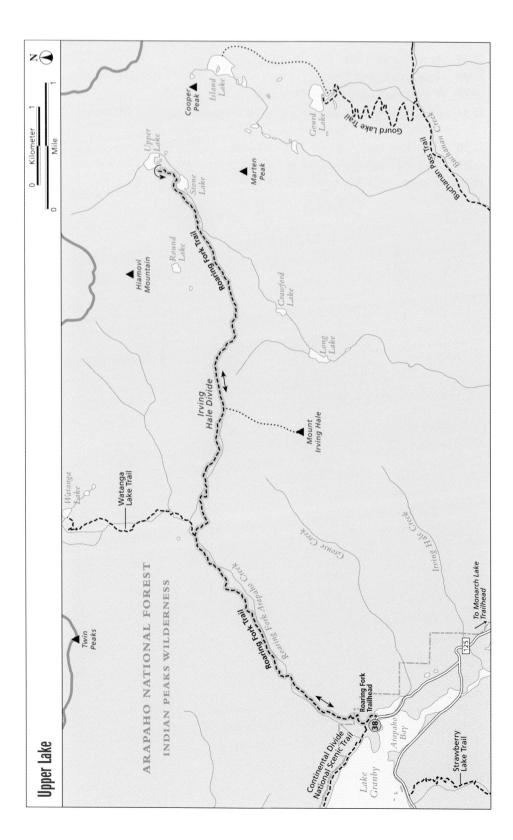

Upper Lake

Twin Peaks

ARAPAHO NATIONAL FOREST

INDIAN PEAKS WILDERNESS

Watanga Lake

Watanga Lake Trail

Hiamovi Mountain

Round Lake

Roaring Fork Arapaho Creek

Roaring Fork Trail

Irving Hale Divide

Mount Irving Hale

Crawford Lake

Long Lake

Stone Lake

Upper Lake

Cooper Peak

Island Lake

Marten Peak

Gourd Lake

Gourd Lake Trail

Buchanan Pass Trail

Buchanan Creek

Grouse Creek

Irving Hale Creek

Roaring Fork Trail

Roaring Fork Trailhead

38

Lake Granby

Arapaho Bay

Continental Divide National Scenic Trail

Strawberry Lake Trail

125

To Monarch Lake Trailhead

N

0   Kilometer   1

0   Mile   1

10.35	Arrive at Crawford Lake.
10.75	Arrive at Long Lake.
12.65	Stumble onto Cascade Creek Trail. Turn right.
12.25	Reach the junctions of Cascade Creek and Buchanan Pass trails. Bear right toward Monarch Lake.
13.10	Leave Indian Peaks Wilderness at Monarch Lake.
13.85	Arrive at Monarch Lake Trailhead. Walk along road toward Roaring Fork Trailhead.
15.85	Arrive back at the Roaring Fork Trailhead.

39 Gourd Lake

On a map, Gourd Lake has an outline resembling a gourd enough to justify the name.

Start: Monarch Lake Trailhead
Hiking time: About 14 hours
Distance: 16.32 miles out and back
Difficulty: Difficult
Trail surface: Dirt
Best season: Summer
Other trail users: Equestrians
Canine compatibility: Dogs are permitted on handheld, 6-foot leashes
Fees: A parking fee or interagency recreational area pass. Permit is required for camping

Trail contacts: USDA Forest Service, Sulphur Ranger District, PO Box 10, 9 Ten Mile Dr., Granby CO 80446; (970) 887-4100; fs.usda. gov/arp
Maps: Trails Illustrated Indian Peaks Gold Hill; USGS Monarch Lake, Isolation Peak
Highlights: Monarch Lake, Gourd Lake
Wildlife: Moose, mule deer, red squirrel, mountain chickadee, osprey at Monarch Lake.
Monarch Lake Trailhead elevation: 8,346 feet
Gourd Lake elevation: 10,800 feet

Finding the trailhead: From the north side of the town of Granby at the intersection of US Hwy. 40 and 34, drive north 5.4 miles and turn east onto Arapaho Bay Road. The turn to Arapaho Bay is about 11 miles south of Grand Lake on Hwy. 34. Drive 8.8 miles along the south shore of Lake Granby and turn right for 1.0 miles to Monarch Lake Trailhead. **GPS:** N40° 06' .39"/W105° 44' .48"

The Hike

To trek to Gourd Lake, leave Monarch Lake Trailhead to follow the Cascade Creek Trail, branching left around the lake beyond the east end of Monarch Lake willow wetlands are watered by Buchanan Creek. Continue left where a trail circling Monarch Lake to link with the Arapaho Pass Trail turns right. After a series of switchbacks between two fairly level stretches, Cascade Creek Trail heads right, and Buchanan Pass Trail proceeds left along Buchanan Creek. Shortly after the switchbacks, an easy-to-miss track descends from Hell Canyon along the creek from Long Lake. A bridge crosses this creek a few yards from where this track comes down. It is possible to ascend this track into Hell Canyon, but mostly it is used as a way to descend from the canyon accessed over Hell Canyon Divide.

For more than a level mile beyond the bridge, the Cascade Creek Trail advances to a trail junction where the Buchanan Pass Trail heads left, soon paralleling Buchanan Creek at a mild grade for almost 2 miles. The grade is not mild from the trail junction where the Gourd Lake Trail climbs left from the Buchanan Pass Trail. But excellently engineered 2 miles of switchbacks greatly aid hikers to reach the lake, 1280 feet higher than the junction.

The view east to Paiute Peak is very dramatic, although strangely more so from near the bottom of the trail. From where a switchback cuts west, a few steps beyond the end of the switchback, aspen frame Paiute. Happily, afternoon light, when hikers

Gourd Lake reflects its rocky shore.

are likely to arrive, is best. Further up countless switchbacks, the view broadens to include the double top of Mount Toll to the left of Paiute and Thunderbolt Peak across the Buchanan Creek valley to the south.

The trail reaches the "neck" of Gourd Lake (also the outlet) before emerging from forest to view the main body at the shore, most striking from the east shore. The cliffs of Marten Peak and Cooper Peak, from which glaciers flowed to scoop out Gourd Lake, are not visible. They are hidden by another dramatic but unnamed cirque wall.

Miles and Directions

0.0	Begin at Monarch Lake Trailhead.
1.6	Reach the junction of Cascade Creek Trail and Arapaho Pass Trail. Bear left.
2.05	The Buchanan Pass Trail bears left from the Cascade Creek Trail. Head left up the Buchanan Pass Trail along Buchanan Creek.
6.0	Gourd Lake Trail cuts sharply left from Buchanan Pass Trail and climbs.
8.16	Arrive at Gourd Lake.
16.32	Arrive back at the Monarch Lake Trailhead.

Gourd Lake

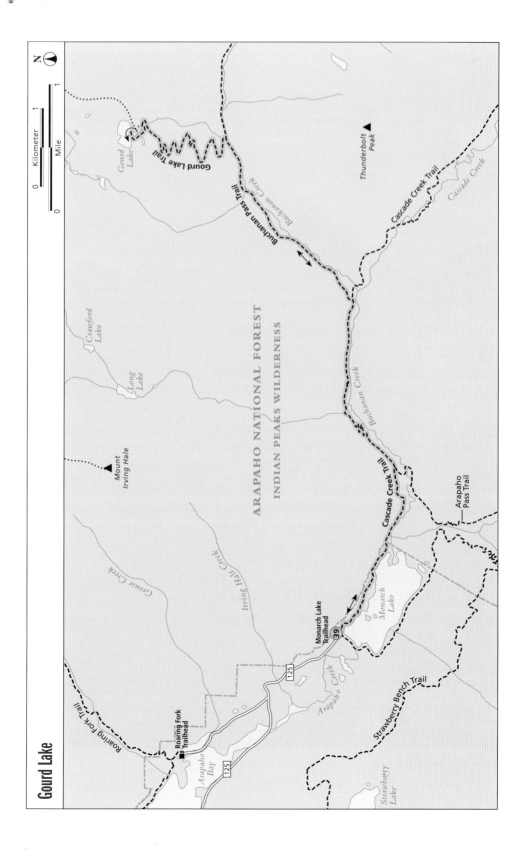

Roaring Fork Trail

Roaring Fork Trailhead

Arapaho Bay

125

125

Arapaho Creek

Monarch Lake Trailhead

39

Monarch Lake

Strawberry Bench Trail

Strawbogy Lake

Arapaho Pass Trail

Cascade Creek Trail

Cascade Creek Trail

Cascade Creek

Buchanan Creek

Buchanan Creek

Buchanan Pass Trail

Gourd Lake Trail

Gourd Lake

Grouse Creek

Irving Hale Creek

▲ **Mount Irving Hale**

Long Lake

Crawford Lake

ARAPAHO NATIONAL FOREST

INDIAN PEAKS WILDERNESS

▲ **Thunderbolt Peak**

N

Kilometer

0   1

Mile

0   1

Quaking aspen in fall frame Paiute Peak from Gourd Lake Trail.

40 Fox Park

Fox Park is a hanging valley along Buchanan Creek.

Start: Monarch Lake Trailhead
Hiking time: About 14 hours
Distance: 16.32 miles out and back
Difficulty: Difficult
Trail surface: Dirt
Best season: Summer
Other trail users: Equestrians
Canine compatibility: Dogs are permitted on handheld, 6-foot leashes
Fees: A parking fee or interagency recreational area pass. Permit is required for camping

Trail contacts: USDA Forest Service, Sulphur Ranger District, PO Box 10, 9 Ten Mile Dr., Granby CO 80446; (970) 887-4100; fs.usda.gov/arp
Maps: Trails Illustrated Indian Peaks Gold Hill; USGS Monarch Lake, Isolation Peak
Highlights: Monarch Lake, Gourd Lake
Wildlife: Moose, mule deer, red squirrel, mountain chickadee, osprey at Monarch Lake.
Monarch Lake Trailhead elevation: 8,346 feet
Gourd Lake elevation: 10,800 feet
Fox Park elevation: 10,437 feet

Finding the trailhead: From the north side of the town of Granby at the intersection of US Hwy. 40 and 34, drive north 5.4 miles and turn east onto Arapaho Bay Road. The turn to Arapaho Bay is about 11 miles south of Grand Lake on Hwy. 34. Drive 8.8 miles along the south shore of Lake Granby and turn right for 1 mile to Monarch Lake Trailhead. **GPS:** N40° 06' .39"/W105° 44' .48"

The Hike

The Buchanan Pass Trail beyond the junction with the Gourd Lake Trail (see Hike 39) follows gently up Buchanan Creek until switchbacks lift it to an inevitable higher level into Fox Park. The detour to Gourd Lake is rightly tempting, but descending from Gourd Lake 1,280 feet to the Buchanan Pass Trail to either visit Fox Park or climb beyond to the pass involves an intimidating loss and regaining of altitude.

There is a better way. From a long forested ridge next to Gourd Lake's southeastern shore, an informal, but mostly clear trail leads to a meadow just above Fox Park. Sometimes the path climbs steeply in order that hikers do not have to cross steep rock. Elsewhere, the path crosses avalanche runs that can be dangerous in spring. Where snow does not melt until early autumn, the path disappears.

However, most of the path is a treasure of subalpine flowers and open views up Thunderbolt Creek to Mount Toll and Paiute Peak. Finally, the path disappears into a marshy meadow watered by Buchanan Creek with better views than those from the Buchanan Pass Trail in Fox Park, a short way below. The Buchanan Pass Trail, rising very distinctly from Fox Park to the pass, is less difficult than it looks but not much.

Marsh opens Continental Divide view above Fox Park.

Miles and Directions

0.0   Begin at Monarch Lake Trailhead.

1.6   Reach the junction of Cascade Creek Trail and Arapaho Pass Trail. Bear left.

2.05   The Buchanan Pass Trail bears left from the Cascade Creek Trail. Head left up the Buchanan Pass Trail along Buchanan Creek.

6.0   Gourd Lake Trail cuts sharply left from Buchanan Pass Trail and climbs.

8.16   Arrive at Gourd Lake.

9.66   Arrive at Fox Park. Return via Buchanan Pass Trail to Monarch Lake Trailhead.

17.41   Arrive back at the Monarch Lake Trailhead.

Fox Park

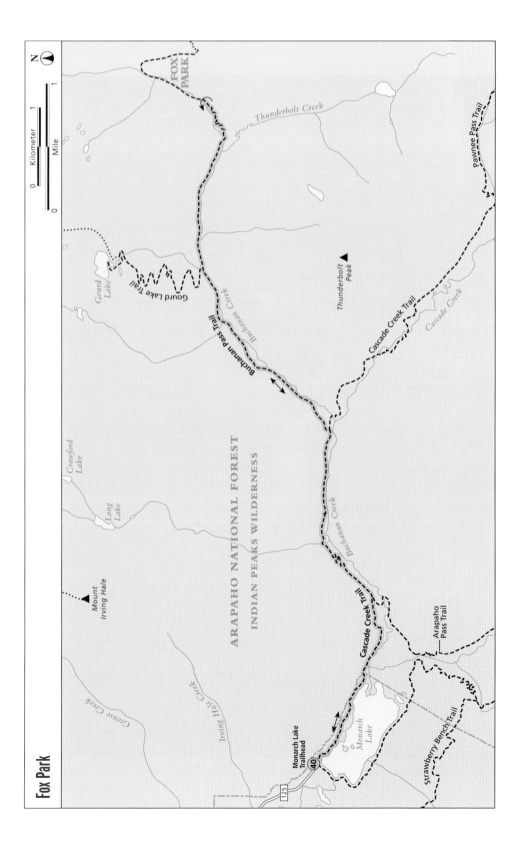

N

Kilometer
0   1

Mile
0   1

Grouse Creek

Mount
Irving Hale

Crawford
Lake

Long
Lake

Gourd
Lake

Gourd Lake Trail

Buchanan Pass Trail

Thunderbolt Creek

FOX
PARK

ARAPAHO NATIONAL FOREST

INDIAN PEAKS WILDERNESS

Buchanan Creek

Thunderbolt
Peak

Cascade Creek Trail

Cascade Creek

Pawnee Pass Trail

Irving Hale Creek

Cascade Creek Trail

Buchanan Creek

Arapaho
Pass Trail

Monarch Lake
Trailhead

40

125

Monarch
Lake

Strawberry Bench Trail

Baby red fox poses in a grassy meadow.

PARKS

In Colorado, parks identify different types of land, which often confuses visitors. The national parks in Colorado were set aside by Congress to preserve important natural or historic sites. Rocky Mountain National Park's main purpose is to preserve wild lands and its wild creatures. In that regard, it differs little from Indian Peaks Wilderness, although hunting is permitted in Indian Peaks. There are state and county parks which serve the same preservation purpose. Other state and municipal parks, however, are heavily developed for human recreation. Parks sometimes identify human communities or towns.

Other parks are natural features: unforested valleys surrounded by mountains. Some, like Fox Park, are relatively small. Others, like Middle Park, North Park, South Park, and the San Luis Valley, are very large. At times, parks overlap each other. For example, Bond Park is a municipal park within the village of Estes Park, adjacent to Rocky Mountain National Park, which contains Paradise Park Research Natural Area, managed with particular care by the National Park Service to preserve its environment unaffected by humans. And none of this covers ways in which park is used as a verb.

Fox Park is the floor of a hanging valley. When ice age glaciers filled the river valleys of Indian Peaks, some glaciers were coincidentally more massive than others. Hence, the larger glacier flowing along the Thunderbolt Creek valley cut the downhill edge from the end of the glacier and valley from Buchanan Creek. When the moving ice melted, Fox Park was left 700 feet higher than the valley cut by the Thunderbolt Creek glacier.

As you approach Buchanan Creek in Fox Park, you might notice pathways through the grass, much narrower and less clear than those used by humans. Red foxes wear hunting trails by following them night after night and always live close to water. Very lucky hikers might see a fox in the long evenings of summer. Clearly, someone did and gave the park its name.

41 Pawnee Lake

Pawnee Lake is a very scenic landmark along the Pawnee Pass Trail below Pawnee Peak.

Start: Monarch Lake Trailhead
Hiking time: About 14 hours
Distance: 16.5 miles out and back
Difficulty: Difficult
Trail surface: Dirt
Best season: Summer
Other trail users: Hikers only
Canine compatibility: Dogs are permitted on handheld, 6-foot leashes
Fees: A parking fee or interagency recreational area pass. Permit is required for camping

Trail contacts: USDA Forest Service, Sulphur Ranger District, PO Box 10, 9 Ten Mile Dr., Granby CO 80446; (970) 887-4100; fs.usda, gov/arp
Maps: Trails Illustrated Indian Peaks Gold Hill; USGS Monarch Lake, Isolation Peak
Highlights: Waterfalls along Cascade Creek Trail, Lone Eagle Peak, Pawnee Lake
Wildlife: Mule deer, red squirrel, mountain chickadee, dipper
Monarch Lake elevation: 8,346 feet
Pawnee Lake elevation: 10,840 feet

Finding the trailhead: From the north side of the town of Granby, at the intersection of US Hwy. 40 and 34, drive north 5.4 miles and turn east onto Arapaho Bay Road. The turn to Arapaho Bay is about 11 miles south of Grand Lake on Hwy. 34. Drive 8.8 miles along the south shore of Lake Granby and turn right for 1 mile to Monarch Lake Trailhead. **GPS:** N40° 06' .39"/ W105° 44' .48"

The Hike

Tucked below Pawnee Pass and Pawnee Peak, Pawnee Lake is visited mostly by hikers traversing the pass. The fame of Crater and Mirror Lakes is justified and may attract more visitors, but Pawnee Lake, only a 2-mile detour from the Crater Lake Trail, justifies a side trip to see its picturesque spires on the slopes of Pawnee Peak. The views from the Pawnee Pass Trail below the lake rival those from Mirror Lake, especially during yellow aspen season (see front cover).

From where the Buchanan Pass Trail (see hikes 39 and 40) branches left along Buchanan Creek, the Cascade Creek Trail branches right a little more than 4 miles from Monarch Lake Trailhead. A level walk along the Cascade Creek for 0.15 mile leads to a bridge over Buchanan Creek. Beyond the bridge, a short stretch with one switchback climbs steeply to the rim of a canyon containing Cascade Creek. The grade is less steep as the trail passes amid those lodgepole pines left from bark beetle attack.

Beyond another bridge, a marshy area demonstrates a midway succession of plants from beaver pond to forest. Upstream from the old beaver workings, Cascade Creek displays how it got its name. So many falls line the creek that they discourage individual names. The trail itself is a destination more than a route to views of lakes and peaks.

Autumn snow dusts Mount Achonee and Pawnee Lake.

Many tight switchbacks ease the way along the cascades. Various spurs lead to viewpoints of the whitewater spectacles. Hikers regrettably pressed for time can keep to the right on the main trail. Near the next level stretch, the path bends left to cross the creek again over water-smoothed rock above particularly scenic falls.

Yet another steep trail section levels where Cascade Creek seems relaxed, winding through ancient beaver ponds before plunging down through falls. Aspen have established groves amid boulder-covered slopes above on the left. Departing from the creek, the trail climbs along a sunny south-facing slope.

The shade of Engelmann spruce and subalpine fir announce a crossing of Pawnee Creek. A bit of winding path leads to a trail junction where the Crater Lake trail branches right some 7 miles from Monarch Lake. From the junction, the Pawnee Pass Trail cuts back over Pawnee Creek toward Pawnee Lake. Just beyond the crossing, yet more switchbacks weave among aspens and Engelmann spruce that frame views of very pointy Lone Eagle Peak with Peck and Fair Glaciers on either side. This view is pictured on the cover.

Similarly, spectacular visions delight hikers following the trail east along Pawnee Creek. The last viewpoint of Lone Eagle and company is from a rock-filled avalanche slope, beyond which the trial climbs through spruces and firs. A cairn marks the short spur leading right from the Pawnee Pass Trail into the Pawnee Lake cirque with the lake framed by forest; rock spires above are satisfyingly jagged. Beyond the lake, the Pawnee Pass Trail snakes very steeply through admirable switchbacks to the Continental Divide.

Pawnee Lake is framed by stone spires on the flank of Pawnee Peak west of Pawnee Pass.

Miles and Directions

- **0.0** Set out from Monarch Lake Trailhead.
- **1.6.** Reach the junction of the Arapaho Pass Trail and Cascade Creek Trail. Bear left.
- **4.0** Buchanan Pass Trail branches from Cascade Creek Trail. Bear right.
- **7.0** Above switchbacks, Crater Lake Trail forks right and Pawnee Pass Trail left. Take Pawnee Pass Trail.
- **8.25** A cairn marks the short spur to Pawnee Lake.
- **16.5** Arrive back at the Monarch Lake Trailhead.

Pawnee Lake

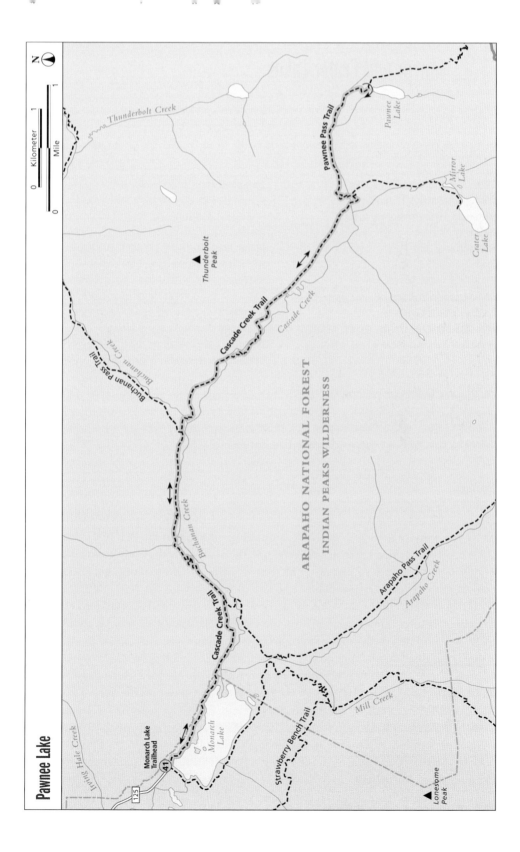

Thunderbolt Creek

Thunderbolt Peak

Buchanan Creek

Buchanan Pass Trail

Cascade Creek Trail

Cascade Creek

Pawnee Pass Trail

Pawnee Lake

Mirror Lake

Crater Lake

ARAPAHO NATIONAL FOREST

INDIAN PEAKS WILDERNESS

Arapaho Pass Trail

Arapaho Creek

Mill Creek

Strawberry Bench Trail

Monarch Lake Trailhead

Monarch Lake

Cascade Creek Trail

Buchanan Creek

Hying Hale Creek

Lonesome Peak

N

0   Kilometer   1

0   Mile   1

42 Mirror and Crater Lakes

Despite its length, the trail to Mirror and Crater lakes may be the most popular on the west side of Indian Peaks because very sharp Lone Eagle Peak reflected in Mirror Lake (hence the lake's unimaginative name) is one of the most famous views in Colorado.

Start: Monarch Lake Trailhead
Hiking time: About 14 hours
Distance: 16.5 miles out and back
Difficulty: Difficult
Trail surface: Dirt
Best season: Summer
Other trail users: Hikers only
Canine compatibility: Dogs are permitted on handheld, 6-foot leashes
Fees: A parking fee or interagency recreational area pass. Permit is required for camping

Trail contacts: USDA Forest Service, Sulphur Ranger District, PO Box 10, 9 Ten Mile Dr., Granby CO 80446; (970) 887-4100; fs.usda. gov/arp
Maps: Trails Illustrated Indian Peaks Gold Hill; USGS Monarch Lake, Isolation Peak
Highlights: Waterfalls along Cascade Creek Trail, Lone Eagle Peak, Mirror Lake, Crater Lake
Wildlife: Mule deer, red squirrel, mountain chickadee, dipper, osprey at Monarch Lake
Monarch Lake elevation: 8,346 feet
Crater Lake elevation: 10,280 feet

Finding the trailhead: From the north side of the town of Granby at the intersection of US Hwy. 40 and 34, drive north 5.4 miles and turn east onto Arapaho Bay Road. The turn to Arapaho Bay is about 11 miles south of Grand Lake on Hwy. 34. Drive 8.8 miles along the south shore of Lake Granby and turn right for 1.0 mile to Monarch Lake Trailhead. **GPS:** N40° 06' .39"/W105° 44' .48"

The Hike

Likely, every hiker thinks the scenery along the hike to Mirror and Crater lakes is worth the work of getting there. There is no disappointment at the lack of a volcano at Crater Lake. Perhaps the magnificence of the scenery completely stunned the imaginations of namers so that no name seemed adequate and resulting appellations, equivalent to "A" and "B", would have to do.

From the junction of the Crater Lake Trail and the Pawnee Pass Trail (see Hike 42), about 7 miles from Monarch Lake, the Crater Lake Trail is occasionally wet or rocky. When the unlikely point of Lone Eagle Peak comes into view above the trees, it duplicates their sky-etching quality. A few hundred yards after the trail crossing of Cascade Creek, the promise of earlier views is realized at Mirror Lake, shallow and bordered by rocks. Peck Glacier is on the right and Fair Glacier on the left.

In 1927, Allen Peck of the Forest Service and Fred Fair, surveyor of Boulder County, both were avid mountaineers. They also were caught up in the national admiration for pioneer aviator Charles Lindbergh after his first solo flight from New York to Paris. Peck and Fair, for whom the glaciers eventually were named, suggested the spire above Mirror and Crater lakes as an appropriate peak when all of Colorado

Caribou Lake sits at head of Arapaho Creek drainage.

seemed eager to have the pilot's name affixed to a mountain. The US Board on Geographic Names vetoed Lindbergh Peak because, contrary to its naming rule, Charles Lindbergh was still alive. The substitution of one of Lindbergh's popular nicknames, "Lone Eagle," satisfied everyone. Most hikers in Indian Peaks today would agree that it is a more broadly symbolic, inspirational name. Remarkable as Lone Eagle Peak appears from Mirror Lake, it actually is the pointed end of a very ragged ridge extending north from Mount George, 958 feet higher.

A nearly level trail along damp terrain for less than a half mile stops at Crater Lake. Without its reflection of Lone Eagle Peak, Mirror Lake would likely be too small to be other than an unnamed pool near Crater. Crater is comparatively large and classically surrounded by cirque cliffs. Lone Eagle Peak is a little less startling than when viewed from Mirror Lake. Mount Achonee is a typically gorgeous glacial sculpture on the opposite side of Crater Lake from Lone Eagle and is 729 feet taller.

Cascade Creek rushes past rock buttress.

Mirror and Crater Lakes

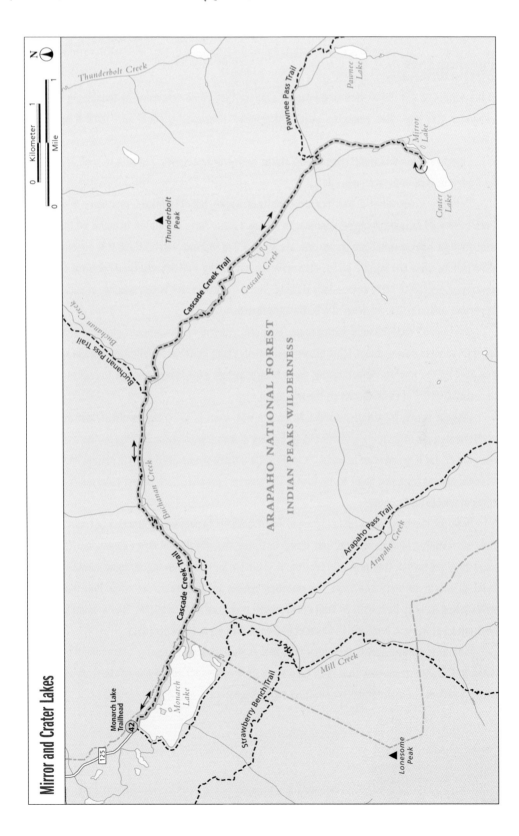

SWITCHBACKS

If the editors of this guide were so inclined, I suppose they could determine by touching a few computer keys how often I use the word "switchback." I reasonably could have used it more often.

Switchback is a fine word: euphonious, clever, perfectly descriptive, and easy to spell. It can be a noun or verb or even an adjective.

Switchback describes a trail construction that hugely benefits hikers who leave Middle Park trailheads for passes on the Continental Divide. I never have attempted to count all these switchbacks. I never would encourage the attempt for two reasons. First, I think it is an impossible task because the infinite joyous distractions surrounding switchbacks would prevent concentration needed to make such a tally reliable. Second, it would risk tragic missing of actually important matters, like the song of a Swainson's thrush.

But even if I cannot count switchbacks, I am very grateful for the arduous pick-and-shovel labor invested in making them. Most hikers acknowledge that switchbacks alleviate muscle ache and burn on the way up. Unfortunately, some hikers are not experienced enough to realize the substantial virtue of switchbacks on the way down.

Without doubt, following switchbacks on the way down is safer, less arduous, and more comfortable than attempting a faster trip by cutting across switchbacks. Staying on the trail is even faster, but if speed is an important consideration, there seems little point in hiking. Pedestrian movement from one point to another in the shortest possible time is best reserved to the track at a local high school.

However, the most important purpose of switchbacks is to prevent destruction of trails and their surrounding landscape. Feet that tramp or tiptoe straight up and down slopes inevitably wear away vegetation that prevents erosion. It is easier for water flowing straight downhill to build up energy to carry away soil. The resulting gullies cut gashes across trails that inhibit walking and have to be rebuilt by trail crews, when trail crews are available. This erosion also destroys plant habitat, reducing the sum of life, color, and joy in the wilderness.

Therefore, cutting across switchbacks is bad. Diplomatically discourage other hikers from doing it. Patiently remember that such hikers are likely not experienced enough to realize the harm as well as the impracticality of cutting switchbacks.

Miles and Directions

0.0 Set out from Monarch Lake Trailhead.

1.6 Reach the junction of the Arapaho Pass Trail and Cascade Creek Trail. Bear left.

4.0 Buchanan Pass Trail branches from Cascade Creek Trail. Bear right.

7.0 Pawnee Pass Trail branches left, the Crater Lake Trail right. Take the Crater Lake Trail.

8.0 Gasp at Mirror Lake.

8.25 Be thankful at Crater Lake.

16.5 Arrive back at the Monarch Lake Trailhead.

43 Coyote Park and Caribou Lake

The "song dogs" commonly appear in brushy areas spotted with trees or along the edges of grassy valley floors such as Coyote Park. Caribou do not appear anywhere in Indian Peaks despite their frequent appearance on the map.

Start: Monarch Lake Trailhead
Hiking time: About 2 days out and back
Difficulty: Difficult
Trail surface: Dirt
Best season: Summer
Canine compatibility: Dogs are permitted on handheld, 6-foot leashes
Fees and permits: A camping fee or inter-agency recreational area pass. Permit is required for camping
Trail contacts: USDA Forest Service, Sulphur Ranger District, PO Box 10, 9 Ten Mile Dr.,

Granby CO 80446; (970) 887-4100; fs.usda. gov/arp
Maps: Trails Illustrated, Indian Peaks Gold Hill; USGS Monarch Lake
Highlights: Monarch Lake, wildflowers, Coyote Park, Caribou Lake
Wildlife: Osprey at Monarch Lake, mule deer, red squirrel, mountain chickadee, coyote (definitely no caribou)
Monarch Lake Trailhead elevation: 8,346 feet
Caribou Lake elevation: 11,147 feet

Finding the trailhead: From the north side of the town of Granby at the intersection of US Hwy. 40 and 34, drive north 5.4 miles and turn east onto Arapaho Bay Road. The turn to Arapaho Bay is about 11 miles south of Grand Lake on Hwy. 34. Drive 8.8 miles along the south shore of Lake Granby and turn right for 1.0 mile to Monarch Lake Trailhead. **GPS:** N40° 06' .39"/W105° 44' .48"

The Hike

Coyotes trot away from hikers everywhere in Indian Peaks except the highest rocky summits. Campers have a reasonable hope of hearing these song dogs howl and yip at night: the theme song of the West.

To reach Coyote Park and Caribou Lake, the west end of the Arapaho Pass Trail starts along the right side of Monarch Lake. Some 1.5 miles later, the High Lonesome Trail branches right. Continue left along the Arapaho Pass Trail to a bridge crossing Arapaho Creek. A short way beyond the bridge, the trail divides again. The left branch links with the Cascade Creek Trail to circle Monarch Lake. Follow the Arapaho Pass Trail right through a series of switchbacks climbing a steep slope through lodgepole pines that have suffered severe attack by mountain pine beetles. The grade moderates along Arapaho Creek above the switchbacks.

Trees and willow shrubs hide most of the creek's course, but side trails lead down to the water occasionally. The Arapaho Pass Trail continues south along the base of a steep ridge. Open spaces along some stretches of creek harbor riparian flowers such as tall one-sided penstemon and monkshood. Soon, Engelmann spruce and subalpine

Clouds hover over Crater Lake.

fir shade the trail. Except in lanes opened by avalanches, thick forest closes around the trail, providing welcome shade for a long walk paralleling Arapaho Creek.

About 3.5 miles from the High Lonesome Trail junction, near an avalanche run, the trail climbs away from Arapaho Creek. After a half mile, the path rejoins the creek where weathering has wedged a chair-shaped rock from surrounding rock to provide handy rest for the weariest hiker. Beyond the chair rock, the forest grows ever more thickly until the trail crosses several creeks at the mouth of Wheeler Basin. As the route steepens, patches of sun encourage growth of wildflower gardens. Finally, the path meanders through the open glacier lily meadow of Coyote Park. Surrounding scenery embraces the meadows with the steep slopes of North and South Arapaho Peaks. Mount George and Apache Peak define the northern horizon. Arapaho Creek waters the heart of the park.

The trail continues through fairly moderate grades, with one notable exception where a set of switchbacks provides a boost to higher meadows through which Arapaho Creek flows from Caribou Lake. The lake sits below Caribou Pass in a bowl defined by Satanta Peak and Arapaho Pass. A short spur right leads to the lakeshore, presenting an intimidating view of the endless switchbacks of a trail of loose rocks to Arapaho Pass.

The people for whom Indian Peaks were named respected their coyote neighbors, often key characters in stories about how things came to be as they are.

Young mule deer grazes amid glacier lilies.

Coyote Park is a grassy meadow in upper Arapaho Creek Valley.

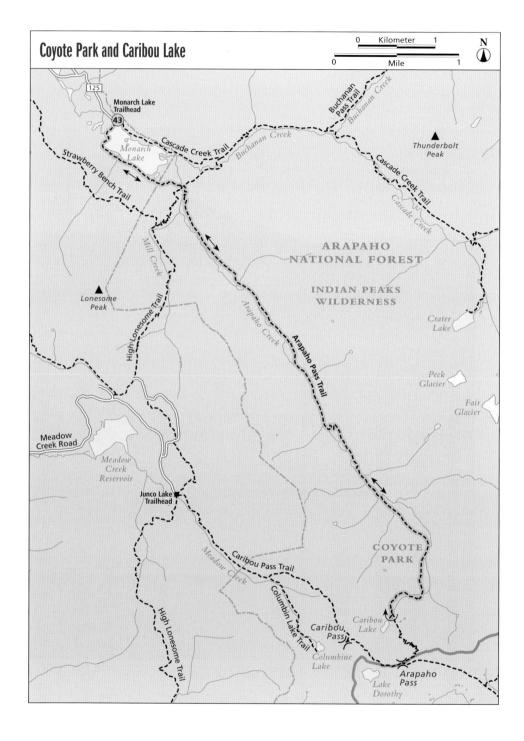

Coyote Park and Caribou Lake

125

Monarch Lake
Trailhead

43

Monarch
Lake

Cascade Creek Trail

Buchanan Creek

Buchanan
Pass Trail

Buchanan Creek

Thunderbolt
Peak

Cascade Creek Trail

Cascade Creek

Strawberry Bench Trail

ARAPAHO
NATIONAL FOREST

INDIAN PEAKS
WILDERNESS

Mill Creek

Lonesome
Peak

High Lonesome Trail

Arapaho Creek

Arapaho Pass Trail

Crater
Lake

Peck
Glacier

Fair
Glacier

Meadow
Creek Road

Meadow
Creek
Reservoir

Junco Lake
Trailhead

Caribou Pass Trail

Meadow Creek

COYOTE
PARK

High Lonesome Trail

Columbin Lake Trail

Caribou
Pass

Caribou
Lake

Columbine
Lake

Lake
Dorothy

Arapaho
Pass

Miles and Directions

0.0   Trek away from Monarch Lake Trailhead, following the west side of the lake.

1.6   Keep hiking ahead where High Lonesome Trail cuts to the right.

1.8   Cross Arapaho Creek and cut sharply right on the Arapaho Pass Trail.

5.3   Arapaho Pass Trail climbs away from Arapaho Creek.

5.7   Trail rejoins creek near a chair-shaped rock.

6.4   The path of avalanches opens at mouth of Wheeler Basin.

7.4   Admire wildflowers in Coyote Park.

9.5   Celebrate arrival at Caribou Lake. Best campsite is just below tree line near the lake.

19.0 Arrive back at Monarch Lake Trailhead.

44 Satanta Peak

Satanta Peak offers a stunning view of the Arapaho Creek valley.

Start: Junco Lake Trailhead
Hiking time: About 8 hours
Distance: 7.6 miles out and back
Difficulty: Difficult
Trail surface: Dirt
Best season: Summer
Other trail users: Equestrians
Canine compatibility: Dogs are permitted on handheld, 6-foot leashes
Fees and permits: A parking fee or interagency recreational area pass. Permits are required for camping
Trail contacts: USDA Forest Service, Sulphur Ranger District, PO Box 10, 9 Ten Mile Dr.,

Granby CO 80446; (970) 887-4100; fs. usda.gov/ arp
Maps: Trails Illustrated Indian Peaks Gold Hill (incorrectly spells Satanta); USDA Monarch Lake (correct spelling)
Highlights: Wildflowers, Caribou Pass, Satanta Peak
Wildlife: Mule deer, red squirrel, mountain chickadee; juncos are common sparrow-sized birds that show white feathers along tail edges when they fly.
Junco Lake Trailhead elevation: 10,052 feet
Satanta Peak elevation: 11,979 feet

Finding the trailhead: To reach Junco Lake Trailhead, leave US 40 about a half mile east of the town of Tabernash or 3.5 miles north of the town of Fraser. Turn east onto unpaved Grand CR 84 immediately south of the spot where US 40 crosses a railroad track via an overpass. Very soon, the road forks; take the left fork and stay on the main road going to Meadow Creek Reservoir (Forest Development Rd. 129). Along Meadow Creek, follow the road as it bears left uphill near the reservoir. About 11 miles from US 40 the road forks; FDR 129 goes right, and the left fork enters a parking area at Junco Lake Trailhead. **GPS:** N40° 02' .4"/W105° 43' .55"

The Hike

Satanta (translated as White Bear, presumably grizzly bear) was famous as a war leader of the Kiowa tribe in the 1870s. But he was not so famous as to keep some hiking references from misspelling his name as Santanta. Historic accounts of the Plains Indian wars and the US Geological Survey map of Satanta Peak do not make this mistake.

To reach Satanta Peak, leave Junco Lake Trailhead (between two branches of the High Lonesome Trail) along an old roadbed that parallels Meadow Creek at a gentle grade. It can be sloppy. About 1.7 miles from the trailhead, the gentleness ends as the Caribou Pass Trail heads left where the Columbine Lake Trail branches right. From the junction, the Caribou Pass Trail climbs steeply through deep subalpine forest shade and flower-filled meadow sunshine. No switchback aids hikers as the trail crosses rivulets, skirts bogs, and passes mine sites. Wilderness beauty, however, diminishes weariness from the direct ascent. Above tree line, 1.5 miles from the trail junction, the view opens at Caribou Pass.

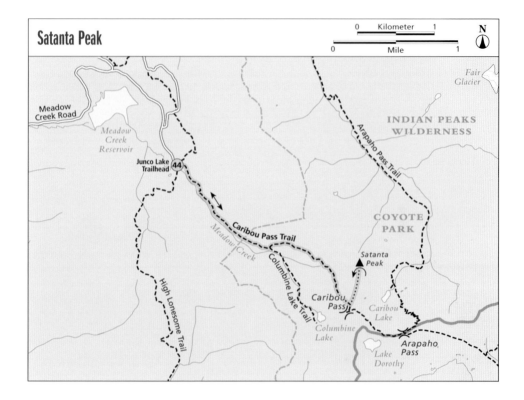

Looking to the east declares the beauty to be worth the effort. The double-humped summit of Apache Peak and Navajo Peak's cone dominate one's attention. About 850 feet below where hikers stand lies Caribou Lake at tree line, accented by small but classic moraines above the trees. The magnificence continues during the simple half-mile hike left from the pass to the summit of Satanta Peak.

Miles and Directions

0.0   Start from Junco Trailhead.

1.7   Old road forks. Right aims for Columbine Lake. Left climbs toward Caribou Pass.

3.2   Arrive at Caribou Pass. Climb left to Satanta Peak.

3.8   Arrive at Satanta Peak.

7.6   Arrive back at the Junco Lake Trailhead.

Apache and Navajo peaks rise above Arapaho Creek valley as seen from Satanta Peak.

SATANTA

In the 1870s, the Kiowa raided Texas, Mexico, and Kansas to kill or capture whites for ransom. Sometimes they sold their captives to the US Army when the biweekly distribution of rations was delivered at Fort Sill Reservation in Oklahoma. The army was prohibited from following raiders when they crossed back into their reservation.

Competing Kiowa leaders split the tribe, some favoring not raiding Euro-Americans and others in favor of continuing the practice. Similarly, the Americans also were split, some (led by agents recruited among pacifist Quakers) favored a Peace Policy, under which the Kiowa would switch their lives to Euro-American economic pursuits and Christianity. On the other side were Euro-Americans who opposed the notion of "conquer with kindness" and believed that Kiowa who ambushed and killed whites and stole stock should be hanged.

In 1871, Satanta, firmly and boastfully in the raiding faction, gathered hundred Kiowa warriors for a typical raid into Texas. On the way, the Kiowa spotted a wagon with a small cavalry escort. They prepared to wipe it out, but substituted their target to a ten-wagon freight shipment driven by twelve teamsters that followed a distance behind the cavalry detachment. Seven teamsters were killed while five escaped, and the Kiowa plundered the freight shipment.

What the Kiowa did not know, but the whites soon realized, was that the wagon that Satanta's warriors had let through unattacked carried General in Chief of the US Army William Sherman on an inspection tour to see just how bad the problem of raiding by the Kiowa was. This close brush with death did not place Sherman in the Peace Policy camp.

As both the Euro-Americans and the Kiowa were split in their opinions about violence, both utilized ambush. When the Kiowa showed up at their reservation for rations after the ambush of the freight wagon train, Satanta was questioned about the raid. He boasted that he had led the raid and intended to raid Texas again. Sherman ordered Satanta's arrest. When Satanta threw off his blanket to pull a pistol to kill Sherman on a porch of a reservation residence, all the shutters on the house slammed open as African American soldiers of the 10th Cavalry trained their carbines on the Kiowa. Sherman conveyed Satanta and others to Texas to stand trial for murdering the teamsters.

Satanta was sentenced to hang, but the sentence was commuted to life in prison. Two years later, he was pardoned and released after promising to quit raiding. While the war leaders were in prison, the peace faction among the Kiowa had control and the raiding stopped. When the hostages were released, raids began as previously. Euro-American society lost patience with giving raiders refuge on a reservation, and the army was released to follow the raiders across the reservation boundary. Satanta was recaptured and thrown back in prison, where he committed suicide three years later. Raiding ended on the southern plains.

Sympathy for Native American culture made a martyr of Satanta. A couple of generations after Satanta cut his wrists and neck and threw himself from a third-story window, a mountain in Indian Peaks was named Kiowa, and another was named Satanta. Splits in opinion still exist. Climbers are banned from Kiowa Peak in the Boulder Watershed, but Satanta Peak, west across the valley of Arapaho Creek, is an excellent climbing destination.

Although Satanta was perhaps named for a grizzly bear, his namesake no longer lives in Indian Peaks Wilderness.

This grizzly bear cub displays white on coat reminiscent of White Bear translation of Satanta.

45 Columbine Lake

Start: Junco Lake Trailhead
Hiking time: About 3.5 hours
Distance: 6 miles out and back
Difficulty: Easy
Trail surface: Dirt
Best season: Summer
Other trail users: Equestrians
Canine compatibility: Dogs are permitted on handheld, 6-foot leashes
Fees and permits: A parking fee or interagency recreational area pass. Permit required for camping

Trail contacts: USDA Forest Service, Sulphur Ranger District, PO Box 10, 9 Ten Mile Dr., Granby CO 80446; (970) 887-4100; fs.usda.gov/arp
Maps: Trails Illustrated Indian Peaks Gold Hill; USDA Monarch Lake
Highlights: Wildflowers, Columbine Lake
Wildlife: Mule deer, red squirrel, mountain chickadee; juncos are common sparrow-sized birds
Junco Lake Trailhead elevation: 10,052 feet
Columbine Lake elevation: 11,040 feet

Finding the trailhead: To reach Junco Lake Trailhead, leave US 40 about a half mile east of the town of Tabernash or 3.5 miles north of the town of Fraser. Turn east onto unpaved Grand CR 84, immediately south of the spot where US 40 crosses a railroad track via an overpass. Very soon, the road forks; take the left fork and stay on the main road going to Meadow Creek Reservoir (Forest Development Rd. 129). Along Meadow Creek, follow the road as it bears left uphill near the reservoir. About 11 miles from US 40 the road forks; FDR 129 goes right, and the left fork enters a parking area at Junco Lake Trailhead. **GPS:** N40° 02' .4"/W105° 43' .55"

The Hike

The blue columbine, Colorado's state flower, appropriately grows along the trail to Columbine Lake. To enjoy columbine and many other flowers, ascend the Caribou Pass Trail, which leaves Junco Lake Trailhead between two branches of the High Lonesome Trail.

Approximately 1.7 miles from the trailhead, the Caribou Pass Trail splits, the path to the pass on the left, the Columbine Lake Trail on the right. Follow the right branch along a gentle grade for some 175 yards when the trail begins to steepen at the forest margin. Beginning at 0.5 mile from the trail junction, the Columbine Lake Trail traverses meadows. A steep climb along Meadow Creek follows. After bending left, the trail meanders among trees and boulders to rejoin the creek and cross it.

Beyond the creek crossing, a short climb reaches tree line, where a level shelf contains Columbine Lake. The trail squishes through wetlands on the way to the lake several hundred yards from the creek crossing and 3 miles from the trailhead.

Many rock slabs along Columbine Lake's shore serve as bases for food and rest. Glacier-carved peaks define the view. Mount Neva, the nearest high peak on the Continental Divide, is out of sight. From a well-defined path a short way above the west side of Columbine Lake, hikers face a trackless mile to an obvious pass below the peak's summit.

Columbine Lake perches near tree line.

Blue columbine dominate a field of wildflowers near tree line.

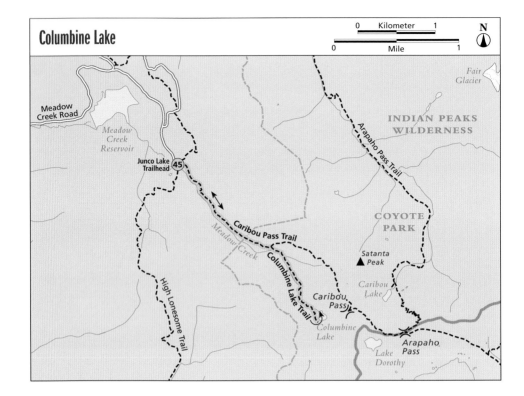

Columbine Lake

0 Kilometer 1
0 Mile 1
N

Fair Glacier

Meadow Creek Road

Meadow Creek Reservoir

Junco Lake Trailhead 45

INDIAN PEAKS WILDERNESS

Arapaho Pass Trail

COYOTE PARK

Caribou Pass Trail

Meadow Creek

Columbine Lake Trail

High Lonesome Trail

Satanta Peak

Caribou Lake

Caribou Pass

Columbine Lake

Arapaho Pass

Lake Dorothy

Miles and Directions

0.0 Start from Junco Lake Trailhead.

1.7 Old road forks. Right path aims for Columbine Lake. Left path climbs toward Caribou Pass.

2.2 Trail traverses flowery meadow.

3.0 Arrive at Columbine Lake.

6.0 Arrive back at the Junco Lake Trailhead.

Blue columbine is the state flower of Colorado.

COLUMBINE

Colorado adopted the blue columbine as its state flower in 1899. I have not yet witnessed the public hanging on the state capitol steps of anyone so foolish as to pick a columbine or any wildflower.

As is appropriate for the symbol of a western state, the blue columbine has spurs. These spurs, when observed by pioneer botanist Edwin James in 1820, identified it as related to the columbine species already known from eastern North America, Europe, and Asia. Columbine spurs are storage chambers for nectar. When insects or hummingbirds eat the nectar from the deep spurs, the nectar-feeders brush against stamens laden with yellow pollen, which the hummer or insect carries on its body to the next columbine cafeteria and fertilizes its seeds. At times, though, an insect bores into a columbine's spur tip, stealing the nectar without serving as a fertilizing agent.

The spurs did encourage enough fertilization to make the blue columbine abundant from shady aspen groves at 6,000 feet to boulder fields well above tree line. Misguided public love for the columbine led to picking and digging that destroyed abundance which modern admirers only can imagine. The Colorado Mountain Club encouraged preservation efforts that produced the state law protecting columbine in 1925. The public seems generally aware that wildflowers should be left where they grow, but expanding awareness has been somewhat frustrated by increased public use of columbine habitat. Therefore, the increased percentage of enlightened columbine advocates has been offset by the increased actual number of flower pickers.

Colorado's Recreation Land Preservation Act of 1971 makes it illegal on public land to "willfully cut down, break, or otherwise destroy any living tree, shrubbery, wild flowers, or natural flora." Prescribed maximum fine is $500.

46 Devils Thumb Pass

The Devils Thumb rises from the east side of the Continental Divide above Devils Thumb Lake.

Start: Rollins Pass (also called Corona Pass)
Hiking time: About 7 hours
Distance: 9.2 miles out and back
Difficulty: Moderate
Trail surface: Dirt
Best season: Summer
Other trail users: Equestrians
Canine compatibility: Dogs are permitted on handheld, 6-foot leashes
Fees and permits: None for hiking. Permits are required for camping
Trail contacts: USDA Forest Service, Sulphur Ranger District, PO Box 10, 9 Ten Mile Dr.,

Granby CO 80448; (970) 887-4100; fs.usda.gov/arp
Maps: Trails Illustrated Indian Peaks Gold Hill; USGS East Portal
Highlights: King Lake from above, alpine tundra, Devils Thumb, Devils Thumb Lake and Jasper Reservoir from above.
Wildlife: White-tailed ptarmigan, brown-capped rosy finch, water pipet, horned lark, pika, yellow-bellied marmot, elk
Rollins Pass elevation: 11,671 feet
Devils Thumb Pass elevation: 11,747 feet

Finding the trailhead: For Rollins Pass Trailhead, start on the West Slope opposite Winter Park Ski Area along US Hwy. 40. Ascent of the 14-mile, rough road to the pass takes about an hour of historic scenery. The road is closed at the pass. **GPS:** N39° 56' .07"/W105° 40' .55"

The Hike

Two glaciers carved the Devils Thumb column from the Continental Divide. Winds prevailing from the west carried ice-age snow to dump in the shelter on the east side of the Divide. After it accumulated approximately 250 feet thick, the ice began to flow, carrying away rock frozen in the ice. The rock remaining between these two glaciers is Devils Thumb. Had wind direction permitted another glacier to form on a third side of the column to cut a third wall, Devils Thumb would be what climbers call a horn. (The Matterhorn in Europe is the most famous example.)

The best route from which to view Devils Thumb is the trail entirely above tree line, traversing the tundra from Rollins Pass to Devils Thumb Pass and a short way beyond to the hiking viewpoint nearest the Thumb. From the crumbled Corona town site, ascend straight uphill (northwest) along the High Lonesome Trail to the Indian Peaks Wilderness Boundary. A short way further, the trail passes a steep trail dropping to King Lake (see Hike 32). East of this descent, a steep snowfield is a hazard. A slip could lead to an uncontrolled slide to rocks that have caused serious injury.

Soon the High Lonesome Trail achieves a milder grade and a pleasant stroll is possible across alpine tundra a short way west, below the Continental Divide. Lakes gleam below glaciated cliffs east of the Divide, but hikers must detour right to look

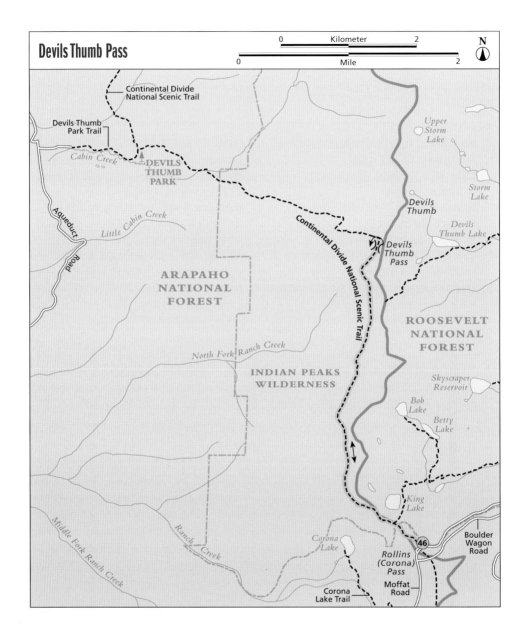

at them. When the trail reaches Devils Thumb Pass, 3.5 miles from Rollins Pass, the view down to Devils Thumb Lake is as good as any offered by detours and avoids trampling tundra.

From the pass, Devils Thumb is disappointingly inconspicuous because it blends with cliffs behind the spire. It is clearer against the sky as the route leads further along the Divide to the nearest view to Devils Thumb.

Devils Thumb stands out from its cliff above Devils Thumb Pass more clearly when hikers proceed a short way along the trail north of the pass.

Returning by the same route is the simplest and most pleasant way back. A second vehicle left at Devils Thumb Park Trailhead provides a circle trip, but the logistics of getting a vehicle to each trailhead can be daunting. More daunting are penetrating beaver-made marshes in Devils Thumb Park. Because the Moffat Road over Rollins Pass is closed east of the pass, placing a vehicle at Hessie Trailhead makes descending to trails east of the Divide an even greater logistical challenge.

Miles and Directions

0.0   Begin at Rollins Pass.

0.3   From the High Lonesome Trail, the trail to King Lake drops steeply to the right.

3.5   Devils Thumb Trail descends steeply to the right to Devils Thumb Lake.

4.6   Arrive at rather skinny Devils Thumb Pass.

4.9   At a viewpoint directly up the ridgeline of the Continental Divide, enjoy a better angle of Devils Thumb.

9.2   Arrive back at the Rollins Pass.

Hike Index

About the Author

Given scant encouragement, Kent Dannen will break into singing "Climb Every Mountain." He was enjoying this song in *The Sound of Music* by Richard Rogers and Oscar Hammerstein at the outdoor Starlight Theater in Kansas City when a passing tornado interrupted the performance. In his great disappointment, Kent resolved to spend his life following the song's advice, somewhere with little likelihood of tornadoes. This explanation of the origins of his books about hiking Indian Peaks Wilderness and Rocky Mountain National Park is close to being true.

Entirely true are his guidebooks *Hiking Rocky Mountain National Park, including Indian Peaks* (comprehensive), *Short Hikes in Rocky Mountain National Park, Rocky Mountain Wildflowers, Best Easy Day Hikes Rocky Mountain National Park, Best Hikes Rocky Mountain National Park,* and *Colorado, Rocky Mountain Country.* His other books include *Listen to the Sparrow's Song* and *The American Wilderness in the Words of John Muir.* He has also served as a hike master for the YMCA of the Rockies and inaugurated their camp naturalist program. Kent has traveled widely for the National Wildlife Federation, teaching subjects such as bird identification, outdoor photography, the history of wildlife in America, and Invite a Bird to Church. The Forest Service has awarded him the US Department of Agriculture Certificate of Appreciation for his "outstanding volunteer service in developing educational materials that help manage and protect the Indian Peaks Wilderness."

The only tornado he has ever actually seen was high above the city of Boulder. He failed to photograph the funnel.

American Hiking Society

Because you
hike.
We're with you
every step of the way

As a national voice for hikers, **American Hiking Society** works every day:

- Building and maintaining hiking trails
- Educating and supporting hikers by providing information and resources
- Supporting hiking and trail organizations nationwide
- Speaking for hikers in the halls of Congress and with federal land managers

Whether you're a casual hiker or a seasoned backpacker, become a member of American Hiking Society and join the national hiking community! You'll enjoy great member benefits and help preserve the nation's hiking trails, so tomorrow's hike is even better than today's. We invite you to join us now!

American Hiking Society